The Last Jews of Kalisz

The Last Jews of Kalisz

DAVID KEMPNER'S STORY OF TRAGEDY AND TRIUMPH

———

Irv Kempner

With Deborah Fineblum

———

ISBN-13: 9781544209654
ISBN-10: 1544209657

Table of Contents

Welcome to His World: The Story of Jewish Kalisz and Why I am Writing This Book

---

YOU'RE STROLLING THROUGH THE OLD neighborhood in Kalisz. And walking beside you, guiding your steps and opening your eyes to a world now gone, are the ghosts of the Jews whose home this once was.

Can you see these streets by morning filled with wagons, their wheels clacking over the cobblestones, their beds piled high with apples heading for market or cans of milk on their way to children looking for their breakfast?

By afternoon the pushcarts are out, overflowing with shirts and scarves, with pots and pans and clothespins and the knife sharpener the housewives need before their *yontif* (holiday) cooking can begin in earnest. Can you hear the shouts of the children playing ball after *cheder* (religious school) lets out for the day and before their mothers call them in for supper? And, as the sun sets, do you see the new bride and groom out for an evening stroll and, later still, the midwife heading home after a long night?

As the sun begins to rise, can you smell the baking challah destined for Shabbos tables around town? And see the factory workers moving quickly through the streets in the direction of the train station, lorries piled high with embroidered finery destined to be adorn aristocrats worlds away from Kalisz? And can you hear the sobs of the mourners following a casket to the Jewish cemetery?

And maybe in the dark of a summer evening you can make out the form of a teenager laughing with his friends in the park.

Even in his old-fashioned 1928 clothing and a language we don't understand (like most of the young Jews, David speaks Polish with friends, saving his Hebrew for *cheder* and synagogue and his Yiddish for home), you can tell by his confident stance and easy banter that David is a natural leader, more comfortable in his own skin than most 18-year-olds.

And as we linger here a moment longer, please notice the body of water flowing through the park. This tributary feeding the mighty Prosna River winds its way through Kalisz's Jewish district. But take a good look now because 12 years from now this body of water will disappear, as if it never was. After the Nazis began stopping it up by dumping Jewish books (along with those from local libraries), Torahs and stones from the synagogue, the yeshiva and *mikveh*, it would never flow again.

But we get ahead of our story. For now let's simply ask David to be our guide. Together, we will enter his world, meet the Jews of Kalisz on their own terms. And, by our simple act of *shema* ... of hearing their voices, we can celebrate them and the life they lived here for eight centuries, a world that remained vibrant and alive until it was stopped up like its tributary just a few short decades ago.

And, as we bear witness to them, we will invite them to share with us the hardships and the pain of that time but also the sweetness of their former lives here.

For David came of age at a crucial time -- the Nazis invaded Poland in September of 1939, just a month before his 29th birthday.

He was by then no longer a carefree teen hanging out with his pals in the park but a man old enough to smell the danger -- though few could imagine the unimaginable cruelties in store for them -- as well as any Jew could in that place and that time.

I know this because David Kempner was my father and, what happened to my family in the 20th cen-

My Dad was 29 when the Nazis invaded his hometown

tury is what happened to Kalisz's Jews. But, unlike nearly every member of his family and just about every one of the pals laughing with him that summer night, the young man who would be my father would survive the hell that was coming at them unseen. He would go on to live out the life after 1945 in relative normalcy, and, because he lived, he would be among those who could serve as an eyewitness to history.

I am honored to be David Kempner's son, to be able to tell his story and the story of his childhood home, the Jewish world of Kalisz, Poland.

There is an urgency about this now. Today, many of the locals you would encounter on that same street corner where my dad

**The magnificent Great Synagogue inspired
generations of Kalisz Jews**

used to meet his friends may not even realize that, a mere 75
years ago, these streets teemed with Jewish life. Today a lovely
green park stands on this piece of land, but with no sign of the
tributary that once flowed through it or the Jewish community
it supported. With the buildings gone and the tributary gone,
with the Jews themselves gone, there is little left behind to tell
their story.

Raising that awareness among Jews and Christians, coaxing the
ghosts to come out and speak to us, is why I have embarked
on this journey of discovery, why I'm so active in fostering
Polish-Jewish understanding and committed to supporting the

Forum for Dialogue. The Forum is the largest and oldest Polish non-governmental organization that's dedicated to inspiring new connections between today's Poland and the Jewish people. Together we educate teens and adults, Jews and Poles alike, to understand the world of the Jews who called Poland's cities and villages home, including Kalisz. Together we learn how this world was destroyed. It falls on us to help fill in the blanks left by the few terse paragraphs most history books devote to the Holocaust at a time when an ever-dwindling number of live witnesses remain behind to tell this dark and terrifying tale.

Both of my parents were born in Poland, my mother in Radom and my father in Kalisz. Both families' Polish roots go back many centuries. And both my parents somehow survived the darkest evil ever perpetrated. They were a small minority, those able to escape the Nazi net, a net that caught their parents, brothers and sisters, aunts, uncles and cousins, a loss my parents never truly recovered from.

For me, growing up in a home with survivors who struggled to make a new life here in America and weaned on my parents' memories of our lost Jewish family in Poland, I was curious about what life was like for them before the war and of course what happened to my family during the Shoah.

I was also somewhat jealous of my friends who had grandparents, aunts, uncles and cousins to spend holidays and vacations with. Today, when I watch my grandchildren play with their cousins and see four generations come together for family *simchas*, I know how fortunate they – and all of us this side of the Shoah – truly are.

After my wife and I raised our family and I retired from a successful career as an executive at the Gillette Company, I finally had the time and resources to visit Poland. It was in 2005 that I went on my first Adult March of the Living trip. It was the 60th anniversary of the liberation of Auschwitz, and an eye opening, educational and emotional experience to spend the week of Yom HaShoah – Holocaust Memorial Day -- in Poland with 25,000 other international visitors and dignitaries.

That week I became fascinated with Jewish life in Poland and our family's – and our people's -- history there. I've been back no fewer than eight times in the dozen years since that first powerful Polish experience, both on other March of the Living trips and also with the Forum for Dialogue, which I've been supporting for years. Working with the wonderful people at the Forum I was also able to sponsor the first two Schools of Dialogue in my parents' hometowns: in Radom and in Kalisz in 2011. The School of Dialogue is an educational program that aims to teach Polish high schoolers about the history of Jews in Poland as well with their contribution to the social, cultural and economic development of the country and their own towns. Participants explore their town's oft-forgotten Jewish history and culture and then present what they've learned to other local residents through various activities organized within the town.

My hope and prayer is that by increasing the understanding between us and raising awareness among the upcoming generation of Poles about the Jews who once lived there, we can say "Never again" to the kind of prejudice, hate and distrust that created the Holocaust in the first place.

In 2015, my writer friend Deborah Fineblum helped my mother tell her story in "Always Good with a Needle: My Journey from Radom to Redemption." And now in these pages Deborah is helping me tell the story of the Jews of Kalisz with my father as our young guide.

Like my father, nearly all of them are gone now (we are very fortunate that, at 95, my mother Marlene Freidenreich Kempner, is a lively exception). And, despite the best efforts of the Spielberg Foundation and the United States Holocaust Memorial Museum, far too many survivors have taken the history they lived to the grave with them.

Now it is up to us, the next generation, to bear witness for them, to rescue and preserve their story. That is why we have written this book, so the world will know them, what they went through and their courage under the most horrible of circumstances. So they and the world they created and loved so well will never be forgotten.

-- *Irv Kempner*
January 8, 2018

———————

CHAPTER 1

The Story of Kalisz

"God said, 'Let the earth bring forth living creatures, and fowl that fly about over the earth across the expanse of the heavens."

– GENESIS, 1:20

THE NAME KALISZ STEMS FROM the Celtic term *cal* which means stream, or the Slavic term *kal*, meaning swamp or marsh.

But regardless of the exact definition, this city is built on its waterways, surrounded by islands connected by bridges, and bifurcated by the mighty Prosna River. Indeed, Kalisz's waterways would play not only a formative and strategic role in its establishment and prominence over the years, but also a tragic role in its 20th century history.

But for now let's be content simply to be visitors here, strolling over the streets and admiring the sights, and finding those hidden clues to the city's history all around us.

EARLY KALISZ DAYS

Anyone who knows a bit about architecture can see that, though built on a typical mediaeval urban structure, most of the buildings in the city's center are relatively new, dating back only to the 1920s or early 1930s.

So they might be surprised to learn that Kalisz has long been considered the oldest city in Poland. (Keep reading and you'll see that the city was largely rebuilt in the 1920s and early '30s after its nearly wholesale destruction during World War I.)

But whether or not it's the oldest city in Poland – and the debate is by no means ended -- there is little argument that Kalisz, dominated as it is by the waters of the Prosna, is the second largest in the entire Wielkopolska region.

In point of fact, local history buffs will tell you that Kalisz (Calisia in Latin) was mentioned by Claudius Ptolemy in the 2nd century as a city in Magna Germania's Diduni territory and a stop on the trading route known as the Amber Trail. And the preponderance of Roman time artifacts here also indicates Kalisz was a popular stop for those traders enroute to the Baltic Sea.

Archaeologists have also identified signs of human habitation that date back to the Piast dynasty, running between the 9th and 12th centuries. Indeed historians tend to place the timing of the founding of Kalisz as we know it on the earlier end of that stretch, when the city emerged as a provincial capital complete with the requisite castle and fort.

Boleslaw I the Brave was Duke of Poland from 992 to 1025.

By the beginning of the 12th century Bolesław III Wrymouth had claimed the town as part of his feudal holdings. By mid-century it had been incorporated by German law and was growing quickly in every way: population, buildings, acreage and business dealings. Kalisz soon gained a name for itself during this period as a wealthy town and during a feudal land-grab, it emerged as its own duchy under the control of the Piast dynasty.

But with a history of shifting borders and loyalties, a reunited Poland saw Kalisz distinguishing itself for its weaving, lumber and furniture industries, as well as its cultural offerings. An equally great honor: Kalisz was selected as the final resting place of the High Duke of Poland, Mieszko III the Old in 1202.

During the medieval era Kalisz appears to also have been a population and trading center, according to the writings of Mieszko III and the remains of a castle that's been discovered and dated by historians as originating in the 13th century. By 1257, the area was home to a lively trading center. In fact, Prince Pobozny's writings identified the region as one "with two major trade neighborhoods crisscrossed by streets and a central marketplace."

And the city just kept growing during this time. By 1282 a set of city laws had been approved by Poland's Przemysl II and in 1314 the city was elevated to the position of capital of the Kalisz Voivodeship by King Wladysław I.

And due to its trade-friendly and militarily strategic location (It was in the middle of the country according to the borders of the day), King Casimir III (Kazimierz in Polish) was motivated to sign a treaty with the Teutonic Order there in 1343. Being designated as a royal town didn't hurt its standing in the region and the city was granted a number of privileges with a stately town hall erected in 1426.

POST-MEDIEVAL TIMES

The city's prominence continued to grow in the 15th and 16th centuries, especially after the Jesuits' arrival in 1574 boosted its status with a new church. In fact the local Jesuit College was destined to become a center of learning attracting students from across Poland. And, though its neighboring city Poznan was gaining in power and economic prowess, Kalisz was certainly able to hold its own during this period. Its economic development was given a boost by the influx of Protestant Czechs who settled in the area following their expulsion from Bohemia in the early 17th century.

Until, that is, a huge setback occurred in the form of fire. A series of blazes destroyed much of the city in the 17th and 18th centuries. The worst one by far devastated the city in 1792, taking nearly every home, public building and business with it and virtually leveling Kalisz.

But, even against such odds, by the following year the city had begun to rise from its ashes. During an intensive rebuilding campaign (including the area around the present-day Wolnosci -- meaning liberty -- Avenue), the second partition of Poland occurred and the Kingdom of Prussia took over the city.

It was on February 13, 1793 that Prussia absorbed the region and, under its control, growth continued apace. And in 1807 Kalisz emerged as a provincial capital of the Warsaw Duchy. Just a few years later, after Napoleon's invasion of Russia and Yorck's Convention of Tauroggen of 1812, Russia and Prussia signed the Treaty of Kalisz.

But the situation dramatically flipped after Napoleon's defeat in 1815 when the region was summarily taken over by Imperial Russia. This dominance would last for a full century, until August of 1914, the beginning of World War I. It would be an epoch destined to wreak great havoc not only on Kalisz but on all of Poland, Europe and the world. And yet, the intervening century would still see great progress here.

After the defeat of Napoleon at Waterloo in June of 1815, and following the Congress of Vienna that same year, Kalisz was declared part of the Kingdom of Poland and a provincial capital and it grew in importance as both an economic and cultural center. A flurry of new buildings reflected this ascendancy including the Governor's Palace, completed in 1825.

Under Russian rule, Kalisz's closeness to the Prussian border and, as always, its river transportation kicked economic growth into high gear. Waves of immigrants flowed in, including those from smaller Polish towns and villages seeking work but also from elsewhere in the vast Russian Empire as well as Germany. Such industries as textiles blossomed due to an abundance of water to supply the factories and lumber from the neighboring forests to use as both fuel and raw material especially for furniture and piano manufacturing.

THE TWENTIETH CENTURY

Reflecting this period of unprecedented development and the beginnings of the industrial revolution, in 1902, a new railway would begin to make exporting and importing even easier and more profitable for area consumers and businesses, since it was now able to link Kalisz with the larger centers of Warsaw and Lodz.

But all this growth preceded a period destined to prove disastrous for the city and her residents, based in great part on its proximity to what was by this time the German border. Indeed Kalisz would be one of the first cities destroyed in 1914 as World War I ravaged this part of Europe, with some 95 percent of the its buildings destroyed by the end of August, 1914.

The first sign of what would soon be at Kalisz's doorstep that summer was when the nearby border with the German Empire was suddenly closed at Neu Skalmierschütz (in Polish it's Skalmierzyce) and all trains across the border to Germany were halted.

KALISZ DURING WORLD WAR I

The closing of travel was unfortunately a harbinger of things to come. Indeed after Germany mobilized its troops and declared war on Russia on August 1, the "Great War" began in earnest with the invasion of Poland. The month of August saw constant shelling under the German forces commanded by Major Hermann Preusker (though some historians put the blame on a Lieutenant Hoffman from the Landwehr-Infraterie Regiment 7). The Russians, assumedly recognizing they were outnumbered and outgunned, retreated without a shot and the German army – many of them connected to Polish families -- were initially for many citizens popular invaders. In fact Kalisz's Mayor Bukowinski even presented one of the German officers the keys to the city as a gesture of friendship.

But it didn't take long for Kalisz to take down the welcome sign. The Germans began by setting fire to military warehouses, trains and other forms of transportation, followed by a slew of arrests, fires, expulsions and killings. The Germans also demanded 50,000 rubles of "retribution," imposed a curfew and stopped all newspapers from being published.

Historians have since pointed out that, not only was the proximity to Germany a problem, but so was the topography of the region -- Kalisz is situated in a deep valley so the Germans were able to attack from the surrounding hills, engulfing their victims.

With the series of fires being set and the shelling, the homes and stores that were attacked and plundered, the citizens of Kalisz were terrified and tried to escape despite German warnings to stay put or risk being killed. The Germans took hostages of those attempting to flee, killing many of them. The Catholic Church attempted to intervene and some detainees were freed while others were sent to German POW camps.

Less than a week after the initial August 2 invasion, in the main market, an escaping horse trigged German soldiers to shoot anyone in their path. Survivors were hunted down and many of them stabbed to death.

In addition, City Hall was torched and the officials killed with more shootings and mass executions to follow. On August 9 the city was burned to the ground and anyone discovered to be fighting the fire, the Germans immediately killed.

The destruction continued for three full weeks, culminating with the torching of the last house standing on Nowoogrodowska Street on August 22. In all, during those three terrible weeks, 95 percent of Kalisz was completely destroyed including virtually every one of the older buildings and such landmarks as the Leopold Wiess Palace. In fact, the only edifices the Germans would allow to remain standing were a few churches and public office buildings.

The population figures paint a stark portrait: Of the 68,000 residents recorded in the early months of 1914, some 5,000 lived there in 1915.

BETWEEN THE WARS

Poland after World War I was carved out by the Allied Powers from parts of Germany, Austro-Hungary and Russia. The newly constituted Polish Republic was now home to some 3 million Jews along with Germans, Ukrainians, Lithuanians and Slovaks. In 1919, in an effort to secure the rights of these minorities, the new Polish government published the Little Treaty of Versailles (Minorities Treaty).

And, since many of those who'd either been expelled or fled the city eventually returned, by the end of the war, much of the city's center had been rebuilt as best as possible by wartime construction standards. Certainly after the war ended in 1918 and

**The towering Kalisz City Hall has been built,
rebuilt and renovated over the centuries.**

the town was able to cast off German control and join a reborn independent Poland, the citizenry and leadership turned their full energies and resources to rebuilding.

Highlights of the reconstruction were the current market-place and a new city hall which opened its doors in 1925 – the fourth to be built on its site, the first one dating back to the 15th century.

Full recovery would take well into the '30s to complete, however, and as the city was finally back on its feet and fairly prosperous, there was a slew of new troubles looming on the horizon though largely unforeseen by the local populace.

A mere two decades between the wars would elapse before Poland was invaded once again by the German army, this time with a demon at its helm. And, once again, Kalisz had the misfortune of being in the wrong place at decidedly the wrong time.

KALISZ IN WORLD WAR II

During the first half of 1939 the population of Kalisz numbered some 89,000 souls. But after the German invasion of Poland in 1939, though no part of the country was immune to attack, the proximity of the border once again proved disastrous for Kalisz. The city was captured by the Germans almost instantly and with little in the way of self-defense, and was summarily annexed by Nazi Germany into what they designated as Reichsgau Posen. By 1940 it would be renamed Wartheland.

At sunrise on September 1, 1939, a heavily armored German army charged across the Polish border – Kalisz was taken five days later. Attacking from both the air and the ground, the

Germans quickly encircled the country, attacking from multiple directions and strategically decimating Polish military centers and key transportation facilities.

By the third of the month, Great Britain joined the fray, declaring war on Germany and allied with Poland and France. A set-back: Soviet forces, which had a secret agreement with Germany, invaded Poland too. Poland was outnumbered and outgunned; Warsaw surrendered on September 27 and, within a week, the entire country was part of Nazi Germany. A new world war had begun, one destined to last five-and-a-half terror-filled years, leaving a path of destruction in its wake that has yet to fully heal.

Soon Poland was carved into two: to the Russians went the eastern section, with Belarus (White Russia) and Western Ukraine. To the Germans went the western portion including Kalisz. The center, including Warsaw, was also absorbed into Germany as what they called General Government.

But less than two years after this seemingly amicable division of spoils by these two super-powers, in June of 1941, Hitler attacked the Soviet Union and within a half year, Germany invaded Moscow.

History reminds us that, by June 1941, Hitler's armies had defeated and taken over all of Western Europe. This enabled him to direct much of his fire attacking the Soviet Union, a half year before the United States jumped in following the Japanese attack on Pearl Harbor on December 7 of that year, and Germany's declaration of war on the US a few days later.

But two years later, it appeared that Hitler may not have fully bargained on the brutal Russian winters. By the time the snows melted in 1943 the German army was in retreat and beating a path back to Poland. By the following summer Lublin was taken back by the Soviets and Warsaw followed early the next year along with the rest of Poland.

By this time, the Germans were experiencing major losses of life and weaponry, in a slow march to the eventual defeat of the Axis forces in the spring of 1945. Tragically, those years saw the murders of more than half the Jews of Europe and 90 percent of those in Poland.

By the end of World War II, besides the roughly 30,000 Kalisz Jews murdered (more on that in Chapter 5), an estimated 20,000 Catholics were either killed or expelled to remote German-occupied territories or to Germany proper as slave laborers.

By 1945 the population of Kalisz had shrunk to 43,000 – roughly half the number of citizens who lived there September 1, 1939.

KALISZ AFTER WWII

Long after the Declaration Regarding the Defeat of Germany and the Assumption of Supreme Authority by Allied Powers was signed on June 5, 1945 and the Potsdam Agreement on August 12th, requiring German demilitarization and reparations, it would take years of hard work and often painstakingly slow progress for the city to rebuild. Especially since so much of Kalisz had been leveled by two world wars for which it sadly had a front row seat for destruction.

But gradually industry both new and old began to take hold and schools and museums and other educational and cultural improvements were ultimately either restored or instituted afresh.

A classic Kalisz street scene.

In 1975, a full three decades after the war ended, following Edward Gierek's program of governmental reform in Poland, Kalisz again became the capital of a province. It was a distinction that would last only until 1998, however, after which the city was appointed the county seat of a separate powiat within the Greater Poland Voivodeship, now considered part of Wielkopolska.

In 1989 democracy came to Poland, opening the minds and hearts of the populace and priming the economy for new growth. Other signs of renewal number among them the city festival inaugurated in 1991 to mark the anniversary of Kalisz's incorporation in 1282. The following year, the city became the seat of a separate diocese of the Catholic Church and locals welcomed Pope John Paul II in 1997. The population also rebounded, and by 2015 it stood at 101,836, well surpassing its pre-war 1939 figure of 81,052.

But in a city that in the beginning of 1939 was one-third Jewish -- some 30,000 Jews called it home then -- today you'd be hard pressed to find a solitary Jew.

Because what we have not yet mentioned in our review of the history of Kalisz is the powerful turn of destiny of a seemingly minor event, the arrival of the first Jew way back in 1139.

CHAPTER 2

Jewish Kalisz: The Early Years

———

"Then Joseph came and told Pharaoh and he said, 'My
fathers and my brothers, their flocks, their cattle and
everything they own, have arrived from the land of
Canaan and they are now in the land of Goshen."

— GENESIS, 47:1

IT DIDN'T TAKE MUCH MORE than a century after the first Jew arrived
in Kalisz for the city to officially roll out the red carpet.

The first arrivals, most likely on the run from the Crusaders
in Germany or Bavaria, came to town around 1139, under the
reign of Mieszko the Old and well before Kalisz became a part
of Great Poland. Indeed coins found nearby with Hebrew letters
engraved on them have been dated to the middle of the 12th
century.

The first Jewish neighborhood of Kalisz (in Yiddish it's pro-
nounced Kulish) by all reports was already up and running by
late in the 12th century here in what locals insist is Poland's oldest city.

The 13th and 14th Centuries

In 1264, Prince Bolesław the Pious made history by writing a charter that recognized the rights of the Jews of not only the city of Kalisz but those Jews living in all of "Great Poland." Dubbed the Kalisz Privilege, it was the nation's first Jewish "insurance policy" and became a model for future royal privileges. Interestingly, the charter defined Jews as both autonomous in many ways and also subject directly to the Duke. It also served to guarantee the Jews' security, both personally and as pertained to their property, their synagogues, cemeteries and other institutions, as well as protecting their business rights from infringement by other citizens.

The Statute of Kalisz was issued by the Duke of Greater Poland Boleslaw the Pious in 1264 in Kalisz.

Even more fascinating: the charter or statute protected the Jews from accusations of killing Christian children to use their blood for rituals. And it stated that any Christian who leveled such a charge would be punished the same way he wanted the Jew to suffer.

The Kalisz Privilege in many ways was a blessing for the Jews, protecting them and their institutions including the authority of their *beit din*, the autonomous Jewish court system. But, on the flip side, it also defined them as the duke's personal property, unlike any other people. And it levied taxes on them beyond those other citizens needed to pay. These taxes were, in essence, expected to compensate the government for these privileges and protections, creating a burden that would prove increasingly painful over the next six centuries.

The Jews' value to the powers of the land was in large part due to their skills at financing and banking. And the government designed the taxation system to make sure a large chunk of the Jews' income would find its way into the royal coffers.

Not only would the charter be accepted nationally by later Polish kings: Casimir III in 1334, Casimir IV in 1453 and Sigismund I in 1539, but it would emerge as a model for dealing with the Jews for several centuries.

By 1264 Jews lived on both sides of the river. Many on Babina Street, known as Jews' Street, which, even in the 20th century, would retain its Jewish identity and centrality. In fact, on a personal note, more than 600 years later, it's the street where my father David would be born in 1910 and where he would spend his childhood.

An early example of a Knaanic coin.

Heavily taxed but still emboldened by the charter, the Kalisz Jewish community flourished. By the beginning of the 14th century it had grown to the point that it had its own schools and a cemetery which was destined to be functional for centuries, in addition to the synagogues, *mikvehs* (ritual baths) and many other religious and communal properties and institutions.

Indeed the years between 1300 and 1600 were generally speaking a time of prosperity when Kalisz Jews were able to succeed economically, despite the heavy taxation, while maintaining the autonomy guaranteed in the charter. Religiously too the region was distinguishing itself with its outstanding yeshivas bringing in students from across Poland and beyond.

But local Jews were not immune to the Bubonic plague – the "Black Death" -- which tore across Europe, leaving corpses in its wake for much of the 1300s. And since quite a few Christians pinned the blame on the Jews, especially in Germany (where it was widely rumored that Jews were not dying at as high a rate as they were), many Jews from that country escaped these allegations by fleeing to cities like Kalisz.

By the mid-14th century, Kalisz's Jewish quarter was a lively neighborhood, complete with a main synagogue the erection of which had been approved in 1358 by King Casimir III. And, as was increasingly the case across all of Poland, many of the Jews in Kalisz grew both successful and relatively comfortable in their adopted home.

The 15th and 16th Centuries

By the end of the 14th century, Jewish Kalisz was an active voice in the Council of the Four Lands, providing a liaison between Polish Jews and the king. Jews were at this juncture well represented in import-export businesses, moneylending and crafts, as well as brokering cattle, horses and textiles – the latter would emerge as the leading business for local Jews for centuries. It was also common for many locals to travel regularly to Germany to sell their wares at the markets and fairs there.

But there were problems looming as well. Efforts to improve Jews' official rights and relieve some of the burden of heavy taxation made some headway in the 15th century. But not without a steep price to pay. Not only did the church pressure the government to rescind the improved terms but a campaign of fires whipped through Jewish neighborhoods and bribes were often required to safeguard the Jews' homes, stores and synagogues.

In 1555, King Zygmunt II August reaffirmed Kalisz Jews' right to freely conduct trade. Still, the burden of taxation levied on the Jewish community (well over and above the taxes on their gentile neighbors) was taking a serious toll and many simply could not work their way out of debt. They were restricted too in where and how they could live, permitted to rent only six houses in non-Jewish Kalisz neighborhoods for which a family had to pay a special penalty fee. A decade later the number of rentable houses climbed to 18 and a stiff per-person tax was added. Popular professions for Jews at the time tended toward merchants, money-lenders and goldsmiths in addition to the usual array of tailors, bakers and butchers.

Still, the powers-that-be pressured the Jews to function as tax collectors for the government – starting naturally with their fellow Jews. And those Jews in shipping were required to pay particularly stiff fines for anything they imported, notably furs and textiles.

And, despite the protections set out in the charter, there was an increasing number of accusations of Jews killing Christians and stealing from churches leveled at the community. These usually resulted in a spate of desecrated synagogues and destroyed Torahs.

THE 17ᵀᴴ AND 18ᵀᴴ CENTURIES

The 17th Century saw the community buying land in the Rozmark neighborhood where they constructed a synagogue of bricks complete with an adjacent school. Most Jewish business was done at nearby Ulica Zydowska Street – the Jewish Street, now called ul. Zlota or Golden Street, one of the spokes running off the town square.

In the early years of the 17th century following the Congress of Vienna, Kalisz lost its distinction as part of the Prussian partition and was subsumed into the Kingdom of Poland. And the professions at which a Jew could work at this juncture began to be restricted. First up: they could no longer be barber surgeons, on the heels of an accusation that a Jewish surgeon was murdering his Christian patients.

By mid-century local Jews had new enemies to contend with: the Cossacks and the Swedes. These anti-Semites swooped down and killed hundreds of Kalisz Jews and hundreds of thousands across the country – often whole families – while destroying thousands of larger synagogues and *shteiblekh* (smaller ones).

But neither the violence nor the heavy taxation stopped refugees from Vienna and those escaping from the Chmielnicki massacres (anti-Semitic killing sprees originating in the Ukraine) from settling in Kalisz in the late 1600s. Though still considered servants – and even the property -- of the royal families, the Jewish community was given self-rule in the areas of most importance to them – their religious institutions and laws and the authority of their own rabbis and other leaders even over financial matters. This autonomy helped balance the frustrations of high taxes and frequent attacks. And the wealthier Jews were consistently tasked with supporting their less fortunate brethren, a responsibility rarely shirked.

In those days Kalisz Jews supported their families with all manner of crafts, among them carpentry, blacksmithing, tailoring and saddle making, the last two predating the community's eventual leather and textile success. They also raised and sold cattle and sheep.

Nonetheless, the 18th century was destined to be a tough one for Kalisz Jews including a cholera epidemic that tore through the Jewish neighborhood, leaving few families unscathed.

Not all the dangers were medical, unfortunately. By the first decade, the next generation of attacking armies from Sweden was setting fire to Jewish homes and synagogues. And, in 1763 seven Jews, including two women, were accused of a ritual killing of a Christian child. Decapitated and their hands cut off, their bodies were paraded through the Jewish streets.

Increasingly burdensome were the special taxes and fees levied on Jews and their businesses -- one way the government helped protect Christian craftsmen and their often exclusive no-Jews-allowed guilds from Jewish competition. The Jewish community had no choice but to borrow money to meet the tax deadlines at stiff interest rates, loans often held by the local Jesuits and nobility. Bankruptcies were increasingly common. Other restrictions of the day: Jews were no longer permitted to set up their pushcarts on city streets, manufacture alcohol or even sell it to non-Jews. And they could only buy real estate on a few limited streets.

Yet despite these forces, the number of Jews in Kalisz grew in the 18th century through increased immigration and a healthy birthrate. In 1789, the 881 Jewish residents of Kalisz made up nearly a third of the city's population. In fact, a census taken in 1737 placed the province of Poznan-Kalisz as the third largest Jewish population center in Poland.

And within a year of a huge fire taking down much of the Jewish neighborhood in 1792, the census reported Jews occupying 91 houses located between Złota and Garbarska streets as well as a synagogue, *mikveh*, cemetery and kosher slaughterhouse.

Economically, by the turn of the century, a time of Prussian control of the region, Kalisz was emerging as a center of the textile trade, a business mostly dominated by Jews, despite onerous taxes and fees. Much of this growth survived yet another political upheaval as the Russians took over in 1815 – a force destined to dominate the region until World War I.

THE 19ᵀᴴ CENTURY

Over the course of the 19th century, despite acts of anti-Semitic violence, the ongoing tax burden and increasing pressure on the Russians from Christian competitors to restrict where and how Jews could do business, Jews continued to play a leading role in the local economy.

But, by 1800, new rules forbade Jews from charging interest and Jewish peddling was outlawed in most neighborhoods. A group of Jewish leaders worked on negotiating with the city leaders to loosen the restrictions on various professions, with some success in expanding the streets where Jewish peddlers were permitted to sell their wares.

Yet some strange and punishing new laws were introduced under Prussian rule: No Jew was permitted to marry unless he was 25 and employed at a level the government deemed sufficient, and there were new stamp duties assessed on the building of synagogues and Jewish documents of all kinds. Despite the provisions of the old charter, the authority of the *beit din* (Jewish court) was taken away and school children – and even rabbis – were required to speak German and Polish. In 1804 the 2,111 Jews in town, some 30 percent of the population, were once more forced to live in tightly proscribed streets and neighborhoods.

In 1807 Napoleon claimed Poland for the French and the following year Jews were made to turn over all inns to Christian nobles and the government. After 1813 when Napoleon granted equal rights to all citizens, the local powers made it their business to keep the Jews in their place, including continued restrictions on where and how to do business and live. Any real estate purchases or construction by Jews was required to be first approved by Christian neighbors and new taxes were instituted, including a heavy one on kosher meat. The latter was fought by Jewish leaders who argued that most families could not afford to buy meat with such high taxes added on. Inability to pay taxes, including those required to support the army, was punished by kidnapping fathers or locking Jews out of their synagogues.

The next power-grab was by the Russian Tzar Alexander who arrived in 1813. New taxes came with him, including a war tax that charged the Jews double the going rate. At the same time the local prefect, a notorious anti-Semite, pressured the city leaders to require Jews to shave off their beards (especially those Jews renting houses from Christians). But in this case his motion was denied.

Beginning in 1821 the government arranged to protect local businesses from Prussian competitors, and Jews also benefited by being able to export their goods – increasingly textiles -- to

Russia and China. And as train service improved so did business. Exporting took a downturn with the Russian invasion in 1832, but was destined to improve again beginning in 1860 when Russia and Poland united and trade flowed more easily, with a lifting of custom charges between the two countries.

In 1822, the Jewish neighborhood was officially designated as Kalisz's Jewish district, a distinction destined to remain in effect for four decades, until 1862.

By 1827 Kalisz was home to 3,463 Jews, a third of the city's total population of 12,107. And perhaps, because they were such a large chunk of the population, the longstanding and more independent Kahilla (Hebrew for community) was done away with by the powers that be and the Synagogue Council, a body with greatly reduced self-governing powers, was established in its place. That same year a town plan was put in place requiring Jews to live within 11 overcrowded streets, though some wealthy ones managed to outfox the system and dwell outside the proscribed neighborhood. That restriction would remain in effect until 1862. It seems altogether likely that Christian business owners, again with an eye to reducing Jewish competition, talked the Russians into restricting where the Jews could live. Other new rules included Jews being required to renovate their homes in a more up-to-date style, those governing the clothes they were permitted to wear (in this case modern only) and the schools their children were permitted to attend (public only). Once again Jewish peddlers could only sell their wares at markets and fairs and street sales were forbidden.

In 1830 the Polish Revolt was actively recruiting Jews to fight, but they were nonetheless continuing to be taxed for being exempt from military service.

Yet the Jewish community continued to build their infra-structure as best they could. In 1837, thanks to donations from the community, the Jewish Hospital opened its doors. As the city taxed the new hospital thousands of zloty each year to keep the hospital open, the debt climbed quickly, a debt it took many years for the community to pay off.

But worse than the ever-spiraling taxation was a disturbing pattern destined to wreak havoc with Jewish families for nearly a century – that of taking Jewish boys into the army for 25 years of no contact with their families or Jewish communities. The first recorded instance of this forced conscription in Kalisz dates to 1841 when nine Jewish boys 14 and under were abducted for the Russian army. Within two years Jewish men were also being taken for military service. How many of these boys and men – kidnapped from yeshivas, factories or their family stores -- would never be seen or heard from again? That number will probably never be known.

The year 1852 was also a challenging one for many of Kalisz's Jews, between the deadly cholera epidemic and the terrible fires that destroyed houses and businesses throughout Jewish Kalisz as well as a 200-year-old synagogue.

Though in the late 1850s there was another escalation of pressure from Christian businesses to minimize Jewish competi-tion, there was also a counter-trend at work by the early '60s: the Polish National Movement. This movement (and its many Jewish supporters) had a clear agenda of increased understanding and cooperation between the Jews – who made by then more than a third (34.5 percent) of the city -- and their Christian neighbors. This air of expansiveness may have been responsible for the first modern Jewish school in Kalisz, with subjects taught in Russian, which opened its doors in 1862.

And the industrial revolution – complete with an ever-expanding rail service – was a huge boon, allowing the Jewish factories to expand their exporting markets (mostly textiles and especially lace), and keeping many of the local Jews gainfully employed as factory owners, salespeople, line workers and shippers. Indeed, lacework and embroidery emerged as the leading Kalisz industry, one dominated by Jews, and the city soon became known as the Russian empire's unofficial "lacework capital."

Though they were officially given equal rights as citizens in 1862, Jews were largely still considered outsiders. Things turned darker more than a decade later when, in 1878 a local minister whipped many citizens into an anti-Semitic fever. As the attackers shot through the Jewish neighborhood, killing 13 and injuring scores more, the pogrom also resulted in widespread looting and the destruction of homes and businesses.

Economic opportunity and on the flip side pressure to assimilate both continued to mount during the last quarter of the 19th century. As more neighborhoods began opening up to Jews and wealthier ones were now permitted to buy land and build homes in the previously restricted neighborhood near the town hall, this attracted Jewish immigration from elsewhere in Poland and beyond. So much so that by 1875 Kalisz was an astounding 45 percent Jewish.

But in 1876, the town authorities initiated a campaign to redefine the Jewish quarter and many of the Jews – and some of their lacemaking factories -- were moved across a tributary of the Prosna, a body of water that would figure tragically in the history of Jewish Kalisz nearly seven decades later. And five years later another law took hold. That was the year the Russians began deporting Jews who were born in Germany or Austria, a punishing policy that continued

**Even in the best of times, poverty and anti-Semitism were
constant companions for most Kalisz Jewish families**

intermittently for decades, and would cost many Jews lives
during the Holocaust.

One day that's gone down in history as an especially low point
for Kalisz Jews of the late 19th century was June 26, 1878. Rioters,
convinced that Jews had vandalized a church altar, began shouting, "From the rabbi's house Jews were throwing rocks at people!" and an armed crowd tore down Jewish homes, stores and
a synagogue while police looked the other way. An investigation
eventually dismissed the vandalism charges against the Jews
and a few of the rioters were convicted.

Such attacks, though painful for everyone involved and
frightening for the entire Jewish community, did little to restrict
its growth, however. In the 1890s Kalisz was home to two large

synagogues and close to 40 smaller *shteiblekh*. But it was also a time of lines being drawn between Jews both religiously and politically. Indeed the last half-century of Russian rule, as was the case throughout the Russian Empire, found traditional Jews pitted against their more liberal "enlightened" brothers and sisters over issues such as education, business laws and the relative authority of the rabbinate. And the "enlightened" Jew often sided with the government on such issues. In addition, the first wave of the liberal religious movement, Reform Judaism, was imported from its place of origin across the German border.

Here as elsewhere in Poland Jews saw the emergence of the lively form of Orthodoxy known as "Hasidism," beginning with the Kotskers, then giving rise to the Ger and the Alexander

**Communal landmarks like the Talmud Torah
which attracted Jews to the joys of learning over the
years, now exist only in photos such as these**

Hasidim. So many of the local Jews were involved that one of their yeshivas, led by Talmudic scholar Rabbi Zvi Hirsch Chajes, had more than 300 students enrolled.

And the Zionistic movement, which would capture many young minds and hearts in the next century, got its start locally with the founding of Hovevei Zion in Kalisz in 1882, predating by five years Theodore Hertzl's passionate appeal to European Jews to leave their homes and build the Jewish homeland in pre-Israel Palestine.

It's all too understandable that Zionism would take hold in Kalisz with its long history of anti-Semitism. As Edith Gomolka, who was born there in 1926, would later write in her memoir, *Recollections of Edith Gomolka* (Richard Gomolka, 2016), "Kalisz was known for its unfriendliness towards the Jews throughout its history. This anti-Semitism existed long before the war or, to be precise, probably from the 10th century onward ... they looked for any excuse to instill fear in every Jew."

CHAPTER 3

Jewish Kalisz: The Twentieth Century Begins

"In embroidered apparel she will be brought to the King."

-- PSALM 45

1900-1910

FOR CENTURIES VISITORS ENTERED KALISZ'S Jewish community via the old bridge ranging over the Prosna River. For residents too, the bridge was where sweethearts met, where the locals would buy their shoes and Shabbat fish, hear fiery political speeches and have their knives sharpened. Here too able-bodied souls would show up at dawn to hire out as day workers. But the bridge also saw its share of trouble, for it was here that that conquering armies -- the Russians in 1905 and the Germans nine years later – would enter, leaving life in Kalisz forever changed.

And it was on this very spot that many of the Jews whose families had been part of this town for eight centuries would be rounded up by the Nazis. For many, including my paternal grandparents, Baylah and Mayer Kempner, the initial destination was the Lodz ghetto where they barely survived the squalid conditions until the day in 1942 when they were crowded into a train bound for the Chelmno concentration camp, a hell from which few Jews emerged alive. Note: All four of our grandparents were murdered by the Nazis. Born in 1950, I was named Isaac Mayer for our two grandfathers, Yitzhak our mother's dad and Meyer our father's dad. Ten years later my sister Tes was named Teresa Belinda in memory of our two grandmothers, Tirtza our mother's mom and Baylah our father's mom.

If you visit Kalisz today, few remnants of their world would meet your eye, besides the occasional faded sign above a shop or inn with a Jewish sounding name. In fact, where they once made up more than a third of Kalisz's citizenry, you would be hard pressed to find a single Jew in the city today. Unless you ran into a group of Americans on a roots-tour searching for some sign that their parents, grandparents or other Jews once walked these streets.

Something else you won't see here today is the tributary that once flowed through Jewish Kalisz. Not since the day in 1943 (the exact date remains a mystery), when the Nazis and their henchmen filled the tributary with Jewish grave markers, books, Torahs and the stones that were once part of Jewish homes, synagogues, shops, yeshivas and the *mikveh*, the ritual bath. Also included were text books and novels from the city's public libraries the Nazis destroyed.

But why stop up a tributary? It's widely believed that the Nazis' goal was to eliminate the Jewish community's source of water for the *mikveh* and other religious uses. At roughly the same time, they burned down the bridge that had for centuries spanned the now-moribund tributary, literally and figuratively cutting off the city's 800-year-old Jewish community. "The Park Built on Books," reads the plaque that's there now. There were once 20,000 or more Jews in the city, it adds. (Note: most reliable sources place that number between 27,000 and 30,000).

But for now let us visit them during happier times. The turn of the 20th century was actually in large part a hopeful time for the Jews of Kalisz. Growing industrialization brought with it increasingly mechanized embroidery and lacemaking. And a new railway that linked the city with Lodz and Warsaw increased interaction with the rest of the world which in turn fueled a hunger for things previously foreign and largely unknown. This growing universal spirit made socialism more appealing and in 1902, the Kalisz branch of the Jewish socialist party Bund was born. In a related vein, the early years of the century saw the growth of Zionism here, a yearning that had already begun sweeping Jewish communities across Europe.

Jewish Kalisz boasted quite a selection of political parties at the dawn of the new century. These included a range of Zionist ones (inspired in great part by Theodore Hertzl), from the religious to the secular and socialistic. And, since parents usually send their children to schools that reflect their values, the socialist Bundists tended to send theirs to socialist influenced schools while observant parents patronized religious *cheders* and yeshivas, which at this juncture enrolled nearly 2,000 of the city's youngsters. Others chose a bilingual Jewish high school or one of two Yiddish-speaking schools.

For many, a loosening of religious bonds expressed itself through the new Reform branch of Judaism, imported from across the German border, its numbers of adherents growing quickly at this time.

Economically things were also looking up for many Jews. By the early 20th century, Jews owned 32 of the 67 factories in town and, until World War I, they made up an astounding 90 percent of all workers in lacemaking, one of the city's strongest industries. As unionizing began to take hold, even the religious got into the act, with an organized effort that eventually succeeded in obtaining excused absences for observant employees for Shabbat and the Jewish holidays.

As good as this sounds, however, in 1908 most of the Kalisz's 14,318 Jews (36 percent of the city) were laborers or artisans who struggled daily to put food on the table.

What's more, pressures continued to be felt from pogroms and economic restrictions on which businesses and professions a Jew was permitted to work in. Another example of increasing governmental controls: The Russians who invaded in 1905 outlawed Yiddish theaters, a ruling that was ironically enough only reversed when the Germans took control in 1914.

But despite these increasing pressures from without, it was still a vibrant Jewish world that, on October 11, 1910 saw the birth of a baby boy to Baylah and Mayer Kempner.

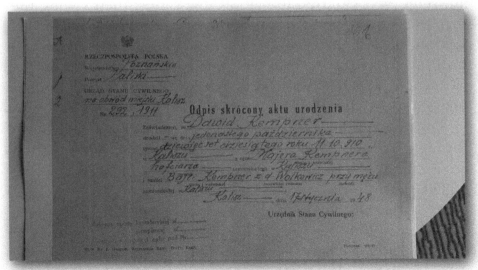

My father's birth certificate, dated October 11, 1910, was presented to me on my Forum for Dialogue tour of Kalisz in 2015

He was their first child and they named him David, after his paternal grandfather. This new baby would miraculously survive the greatest crime ever perpetrated against humanity and would someday become a father himself – to me in 1950 and, a decade later, to my sister Tes.

My father grew up at 16 (it's now 17) Babina Street in the heart of Jewish Kalisz. From the age of 3, he went off to *cheder* every morning where, with the other little boys, he learned the intricacies of Torah and Talmud. Across the street, he recalled, was the city park through which the afore-

My father always said his mother Baylah Kempner was a talented seamstress who made the best chicken soup in the world

mentioned tributary of the mighty Prosna flowed. And, within an easy walking distance were two synagogues, a *mikveh* and the Jewish hospital.

Though in all the years I knew him, my dad tended to shy away from speaking about his early years, especially the painful parts, he did share with us that he once had a little brother named Beryl who was three years his junior. Beryl was ill and bedridden, my dad recalls. He was only 7 when a Polish doctor who came to the house accidently administered an overdose of pain killers that killed him.

Grandfather Mayer Kempner was an ardent Zionist, but his plan to move the family to Israel would sadly fall short of saving my grandparents

THE YEARS LEADING UP TO WORLD WAR I: KALISZ IN THE LINE OF FIRE, 1911-1914

In a classic tug of war, while a new wave of secular learning and enlightenment was sweeping the Jewish world, a counter-wave of religious fervor was also washing over the Jews. Yeshivas and world-renowned rabbis made their homes here, including those representing such Hasidic sects as Ger, Skierniewice, Aleksander, Sochaczew, Sokolow, Kotzk, Parisow and Radomsk. Young yeshiva *bohkerim* (students) from around Eastern Europe would be hosted by local families so they could learn from such rabbinic luminaries as Rabbi Velvel Mozes, Rabbi Morgenstern (who would be murdered by the Germans in the opening months of World War I) and the renown Ger leader Rabbi Abraham Mordechai, who went on to establish the local religious Agudat Israel party.

Just before the war, there was a new uptick in Zionism that would stay strong for decades here. And many young adults made their way to pre-Israel Palestine, facing a life of immense hardship there in those pre-war years.

Despite their religious and political differences, it's widely reported that Kalisz Jews had a tradition of working together to not only honor their common traditions but, in good times and bad, to support charitable organizations as well as the Jewish hospital and home for the elderly.

THE WORLD WAR I YEARS: 1914-1918

This war which was destined to have such devastating impact on Kalisz and its Jewish community exploded into town in early August of 1914. The city's precarious position on the German border made Kalisz a sitting duck for German forces who chased the Russians from town and from power in just a few hours. Though some Jews initially welcomed the Germans as likely to be better to live under than the Russians had been, it didn't take long for German anti-Semitism to show itself in the most violent of terms.

The 33 Jews the German killed and the houses and stores they burned over the first few days after invasion were intimations of things to come over the next few years for the city's Jews. Economically, too, the Germans cut off the Jewish lifeblood by sealing off the Russian market which had been the major support of the primarily Jewish lace and embroidery industry. Until then, lace and embroidery had kept a large percentage of the city's Jews employed and their families fed.

Between August 2 and August 22, the Jews lost much of their neighborhood and market area to German shelling and fires. On Tisha B'Av, a day marking the destruction of the two holy temples in Jerusalem, several Jewish-owned factories were burnt to the ground and hundreds of Jews were murdered.

But even as things looked increasingly bleak for local Jews, others from elsewhere in Poland sought refuge in Kalisz, with the Great Synagogue opened up as a temporary refuge for many of the newcomers.

Still, many Jewish entrepreneurs, even after their factories were seriously damaged, often found ways to continue to do business. Despite the destruction the war brought to the city's Jews and their businesses and neighborhoods, 1916 and 1917 saw a strong rebound of Jewish life and vibrancy.

A surprising air of optimism (tempered by a certain realism about their future in the city) often found expression in a surge of Zionistic activity especially among young adults. It was a passion fed by both the anti-Semitism they lived with daily and the Brits' Balfour Declaration in 1917. This document made Britain the first country to officially support the idea of a Jewish homeland in Palestine, a position they reversed later when effectively blocking Jewish immigration beginning in 1933.

Conversational Hebrew classes and choruses singing Israeli songs were increasingly popular in Kalisz as were Zionistic programs through the Poale Zion movement, Tseirei Zion and Hapoel Hatzair of Eretz Israel. Many if not all were designed to promote *aliyah* – literally "going up" or moving to Israel, most notably among the young who were willing to risk the rigors of the rough-and-tumble pioneer lifestyle – and even the malaria – to distance themselves from the increasing incidence of anti-Semitism at home.

Besides acting as cheerleaders for *aliyah,* several Zionistic organizations, including the Left Poalei Zion, offered night school (mostly in Hebrew and technical subjects such as engineering and science) for young factory workers. This served to level the playing field for many who had been forced to drop out of school as youngsters to support their families.

In the war years, though plenty of Jewish children attended Polish-speaking public schools, many also continued to be educated in more traditional *cheders* as well as a religious trade school and one for older girls from observant families. In addition, the first after-school Hebrew school was established in 1916 and a summer camp also opened for Jewish children with medical challenges.

AFTER WORLD WAR I

Beginning in late 1918, when the war ended and the Poles took Poland back, there was an accelerated regeneration for the Jews of Kalisz. In business, both embroidery and lace manufacturing expanded dramatically as did, to a lesser extent, Jewish-owned flour mills. As a result, there was a growth in trade unions designed to protect workers' rights. Indeed, under union influence, workers began to earn more money and work fewer hours (though still far more than today's workers do in first-world countries). Even street peddlers and other one-person businesses negotiated through their union, the Society of Home. Still, union organizers often paid a steep price for such progress, with the government exiling many of them to Siberia as punishment for their activism.

The post-war years saw the streets of the Jewish neighborhoods more bustling than ever, with a new intermingling of Jew and gentile in cafes and the central market. Many unions brought Jew and gentile together (although others were still segregated), including not only factory workers but clerks, porters and maids as well. And, despite the efforts of the Ger Hasidim and other Orthodox groups, assimilation gained momentum during the late teens and early 1920s.

At the same time, the ranks of the cadre of young Zionists continued to swell dramatically in the between-war years, notably members of Hashomer Hatsair, who often frequented the courtyard of those offices on Ciasna Street.

Indeed by 1919 things once again began to come back to life for Kalisz and the local Jewish community. With the birth of Independent Poland, lace manufacturing and embroidery and now leather work too, were back in full swing with exporting increasingly profitable thanks in great part to having the railways back in civilian use.

In 1918, the Yidisher Turn un Sport Farayn grew to embrace not only sporting events but a library, a night school for languages and science and eventually even a band. And, by 1919 there were two Yiddish newspapers keeping everyone up to date, *Di Jidisze Woch* (*The Jewish Week*) and *The Kaliszer Blat* (*The Kalisz Page*).

Yet it seems every time the Jews begin to feel secure in their adopted homeland, there comes a powerful reminder that this feeling is an illusion. Beginning in early March of 1919, the city's anti-Semitic Endecja party launched a series of pogroms. One of the bloodiest of them followed on the heels of the Jewish community's annual May Day parade, leaving two Jews murdered, many more injured and countless homes and businesses ransacked, looted and destroyed.

In response, several self-defense groups were formed in the Jewish community, in order to protect the city's Jews (who had by now surpassed 15,000 or 35 percent of the total population). And fear of continuing violence kicked Zionism and immigration into high gear, with parents often scrimping and saving for years to send one or more of their children out of harm's way to Israel, America or other hopefully safer locales.

Despite the antagonism in the air, in many ways the 1920s were a wonderful time for my dad to grow up on Babina Street, a neighborhood at the heart of the Jewish community. But what he and his friends could not have known was that, after eight centuries there, they would be the last generation of Jewish kids to grow up playing on the streets of Kalisz. Sadly, most of his cousins and friends would not live past their 30th birthdays.

THE COMMUNITY

But the 1920s, the decade following World War I, was -- pogroms, heavy taxation and restrictive laws notwithstanding -- a time of great expansion when an air of optimism hung over Jewish Kalisz.

As part of the newly independent Poland, Kalisz saw massive reconstruction, especially in the center of the town, an area that had been repeatedly fire-bombed by German forces during World War I.

The Jewish community, representing 35 percent of the city's residents, stood at 15,566, according to official 1921 population figures. The epicenter of Kalisz's Jewish life then was Zlota (Golden) Street, a thoroughfare filled with homes, apartments and the Great Synagogue where Jews would gather to learn or congregate outside in good weather to catch up with friends. And countless men would spend their after-work hours in lively Talmud debate at the Talmud Torah (House of Study) tucked behind the Great Synagogue.

Though the Jews spent most of their time in their own neighborhoods, the '20s brought increasing mixing and doing business with the general Kalisz community. And, more and more, Jewish parents had both secular and religious schools to choose from for their children.

The Kehilla was once again the official governing body for the Jewish community at this time. It was led by the traditional Agudat Israel party which oversaw Kalisz's Jewish institutions including the old-age home, Talmud Torah, orphanage, mikveh

**Like all traditional Jewish communities, in Kalisz the Mikveh
or ritual bath could be relied upon by both women and men.**

(ritual bath), burial society, hospital and clinic, along with the
mikveh and yeshivas where young men received their grounding
in Torah, Talmud and other sources of Jewish wisdom.

Also, since the 500-year-old Jewish cemetery was by this time
filled to capacity, new arrangements had to be made for Jewish
burial. In 1920, the Kehilla negotiated the purchase of land for
a new cemetery. It would receive the remains of, among others,
the widely beloved Rabbi Yehezkel Livshits, who led the community for a quarter of a century.

At this juncture, most of the Jewish neighborhood of Kalisz
was located in the northwest area of the central city, along the
main boulevard, Ulica Nova (New Street). This turned into
Zlota Street and its environs, a neighborhood where locals had
countless shops, bakeries and butchers to choose from alongside synagogues, cafes and residences. Other Jewish streets had

names like Babina (where my dad spent his formative years), Chopin, Ciasna and Kanonicka.

The New Market was also a center of Jewish trade and, in addition to its stationary shops and stalls, was frequented by peddlers hawking all kinds of wares. And the aforementioned bridge, a continuation of Ulica Nova Street that crossed the Prosna River, continued to attract countless Jews daily for both social and business assignations. But as central as these streets were to the Jews of Kalisz, there was a growing trend of the wealthy ones to live in other, more upscale areas of town.

So comfortable did the community begin to feel at this time that in 1921 they voted to risk holding another May Day parade, the first since the attack on the one in 1919. Unfortunately, their optimism was ill-advised -- Polish youth attacked several of the marchers that year with clubs.

RELIGION

The Kalisz Jewish community of the day embraced a wide range of religious philosophies and life styles. These spanned the gamut from traditionalists to the increasing number of less observant and usually wealthier intelligentsia who often socialized with the gentiles and downplayed their Jewish identity. But Jews across the spectrum who had even a minimal amount of income to spare tended to cooperate for the benefit of their less fortunate brethren. This included those who required help with food, shelter, medical care and education for their children, and extending to paying for such life cycle events as weddings and funerals.

The aforementioned Rabbi Yehezkel Livshits, who served as chief rabbi from 1907 to 1932, was not only the undisputed local Jewish leader in both religious and civil matters, but also served as president of the Rabbinical Association of Poland. A proud Zionist, he was a longtime friend of the Chief Rabbi of Palestine Abraham Isaac Kook. Rabbi Livshits' death in 1932 proved a great loss for a Jewish community already beset by increasing antisemitism and economic woes. After his death, Rabbi Menahem Mendel Alter, a leader of the Ger Hasidim, took over as chief rabbi and he too was elected President of the Rabbinical Association of Poland before being murdered in the Shoah along with much of his congregation.

Though there was a clear trend for lightening of religious obligations, Hasidism remained a force to be reckoned with in the 1920s. In addition to the Ger, most of the other dominant Hasidic groups at the time in Kalisz remained virtually unchanged from the previous century. These included Aleksander, Sochaczow, Skierniewice, Kotzk, Sokolow, Parysow and Radomsk. In addition, the chief rabbis of the Zychlin and Wola sects both lived in town. In fact, there was such a density of religious life in those days that those who lived in the Jewish neighborhoods recall the singing on Friday nights was as loud as it was joyous.

In addition to the Great Synagogue where my father would read from the Torah at his bar mitzvah in the fall of 1923 and the dozens of Hasidic *shtieblechs,* tiny (often one-room) synagogues, on the other side of the religious rainbow was the New Synagogue, a.k.a. the German Shul. It was the first in town to introduce the Reform-style choir and organ, and at this time, the congregation was rapidly attracting new members.

**The New Synagogue attracted a large following
to its more liberal form of worship**

ECONOMY

Kalisz's dominance in textiles and garment manufacturing, particularly lace and embroidery with leather now coming in a strong third, grew exponentially between the two world wars. And most of these factories and distributors were Jewish owned and operated. In 1921, three-quarters of the 500 Jewish-owned factories and related businesses handled textiles and leather – the others tended toward lumber, flour milling and metals. Much of this growth can be credited to improved machinery in the factories as well as increased transportation and distribution channels.

At the time a full 45 percent of Kalisz's workers were Jewish and most of them were members of trade unions. Some of the unions (including the embroiderers) accepted workers of all faiths whereas others (those representing garment workers for instance) were segregated by religion. Other Jews worked in the professions, such as medicine, teaching, law and accounting, though those professions were nowhere close to today's high percentage among the Jewish workforce.

And where money is being made banks are never far behind. Two Jewish ones grew up after World War I, the Merchants Bank and the Cooperative Bank, though, like many around the globe, both were destined to go under during the Great Depression.

POLITICS

Competing beliefs and party loyalties were guaranteed to inspire passionate debate in this between-war era. In fact there was a fine, almost invisible line between religion and politics in those days. And the Jews of Kalisz were active in both the politics of the Jewish community and the general political life of the city and region with 11 seats of 34 total on City Council allotted to Jewish parties in 1927. Politically most Jews were allied with the most traditionally observant Agudat Israel (In Yiddish, that's Agudas Yisroel) party, followed by the various flavors of Zionists including the youthful Hashomer Hatsair and the anti-Zionist socialist Bund party.

But the '30s saw a weakening of the Agudat party's power within the Jewish communal rank and file, as the Zionistic and socialistic political forces gathered momentum.

Indeed Zionism was increasingly attractive to Jews in the 1920s. The socialist Zionist party Poale Zion sponsored a "Worker's Home" club, which organized lectures, Hebrew classes and performances and offered its members a library and reading room. And thousands turned out to celebrate Britain's passing of the Mandate of Palestine in 1920. Countless young adults took advantage of nearby Zionist training farms to learn skills preparing them for life in the Jewish homeland and substantial funds were raised for purchasing land there during the Third Aliyah. This saw 40,000 Jews, mostly from Eastern Europe, risking everything to brave the rigors of life in Palestine.

In fact many of these young Zionists bid farewell to their families and traveled to Palestine to live their dream. But it turned out for most to be far from an easy life. The land that welcomed them was riddled with poverty, disease and angry Arabs. But, these dangers notwithstanding, the fourth Aliyah in 1924-28 would also prove to be a lifesaver for many, snatching them out of the way of the Nazis who were destined to destroy Polish Jewry a generation later.

One sad example of this occurred in my own family. My grandmother Baylah's brother Abraham Wolkovitch had made *aliyah* in 1925, moving to a kibbutz near Acco. Two years later, in 1927, during the Fourth Aliyah, he convinced his brother-in-law, my ardent Zionist grandfather Mayer, then 47, to join him there. My father told us many times how his father left for Palestine with every intention of getting settled there and then sending for him and my grandmother. At 17 my dad agreed to leave school and work in his father's small embroidery and lace factory to support his mother until his father could send for them.

But the plan changed abruptly late one night when my grandfather was standing guard on the kibbutz a few months after he arrived in Palestine. A group of Arabs captured him, beat him badly and cut off his big toe, warning him – and sending the message to the other Jews on the kibbutz -- to go back to Poland.

Which is what he did, the tragic irony being that returning to the "safety of Poland" cost him and my grandmother their lives a mere 15 years later. In 1942, with most of the rest of Kalisz Jews, they were taken first to the Lodz ghetto and then to the Chelmno concentration camp where, based on their age, they were probably murdered fairly quickly. In fact, since the Nazis compiled a list of Kalisz Jews who were taken to the Lodz ghetto, any faint hope that my grandparents had been able to escape was dashed when we saw their names on that list.

EDUCATION

But two decades earlier, in the Kalisz of the 1920s, Jewish parents could not foresee that terrible outcome. Back then they were busy choosing from any number of educational options for their children, each one reflecting one of a myriad of religious, political or social philosophies.

Among them were the ever-popular traditional *cheders* to establish the child in the basic Jewish skills. My dad's memories of *cheder* included sitting around a table with other little boys day after day, reciting Hebrew words. "Only after we learned them over and over again did they begin to make sense," he recalled.

In 1922, when my dad was 12, his parents enrolled him in the Mizrachi School, a religious Zionist institution established in 1917. Three years later, at 15, he was sent away for a year in a prestigious Jewish school for teenaged boys, Chachmei Lublin Yeshiva. Founded by Rabbi Meir Shapiro, it was an important center of Torah study in Poland. There he learned wisdom that would give him strength during the coming storm. He often recalled studying *Chumash* (Torah) by candle light as well as the antics of mischievous boys in his yeshiva who delighted in playing tricks on their teachers. The following year, my dad returned to town to lend his father a hand in the family's small embroidery factory -- helping to run it during the months his father was in Israel -- and he later graduated from a more secular local high school.

In fact, at an age when my father had left town for an intensive Jewish learning experience, plenty of other young men from across Poland would come to Kalisz to learn at the yeshiva, the Kalish House of Study. Some crowded into rented rooms but others with even less money slept on benches in the House of Study, taking their meals with a rotation of local families. In fact, many met their future wives that way.

In addition to religiously oriented schools, the Kalisz of the '20s was also home to the Jewish Gymnasium, a high school where secular subjects were taught in Polish along with religious ones in Hebrew. There was also a Zionist Mizrahi party school, a crafts school, two Yiddish schools, and a more secular socialist Bund school as well as a Jewish women's trade school. Yet among the faithful there was a growing concern about the increasing number of Jewish children who went to public school and received little in the way of Jewish education.

CULTURE

Those who lived in the city in the '20s were able to testify to the broad range of cultural offerings, from theaters to symphony orchestras, a lively literature scene and the Shalom Aleichem Jewish Library.

Not only did theatrical companies including the Comet Amateur Little Theatre, founded in 1925, abound, but all manner of performing arts were represented. These included a Jewish orchestra and brass band, a Bund-sponsored drama club, symphonic orchestras and a choir.

Kalisz also was home to such Jewish literary luminaries as Yiddish fiction writer Symon Horonczyk as well as poet, editor and columnist Herszel Solnik and poet Roza Jakubowicz, who would later die in the Warsaw ghetto. In addition, the latest in science, linguistics and folklore was celebrated by the local chapter of YIVO Institute for Jewish Research, which got its start in 1925 in Vilna.

In the 1920s there was also a range of local newspapers to choose from, both religious and secular. The two longtime competing Yiddish weeklies *Kaliszer Lebn* (*Kalisz Life*) and the more liberal *Kaliszer Woch* (*Kalisz Week*) were, however, destined to be overshadowed by *Kaliszer Lebn* (*Kalisz Life*) which began publishing in 1927.

Sports

Kalisz Jews also had a full menu of sporting activities and clubs to enjoy, including those sponsored by political parties such as the Bund and Poale Zion-Right. The Jewish Rowers Club of Kalisz competed against other teams from across Poland while the Jewish Gymnastics and Sports Association, the forerunner of the local Maccabi club, was well known for its gymnastics. Also for its ping-pong team, or so we like to think since my father, a passionate ping-pong player, was its captain. He also played the position of striker on the Kalisz Maccabi soccer team.

1929-1933

But the economic momentum and relative prosperity the local Jewish community had enjoyed in the decade following World War I was dealt a terrible blow beginning in the fall of 1929 with the onset of the worldwide Great Depression. The increasing economic pressures once again saw the Jews cast as scapegoats and many of their legal rights and financial gains eroded during the early 1930s. Upon returning to Poland from what was then Palestine, my grandfather Mayer took the reins back from my dad of the small factory in Kalisz where he and his partner manufactured embroidery material for blouses, curtains and women's undergarments. Like so many others, however, that business was doomed. It closed its doors in the early '30s, a victim of the Depression and governmental policy changes that fastened a noose around small Jewish business' necks.

In fact, as the economy deteriorated, the Polish government increasingly adopted anti-Jewish economic policies, including, as in former years, restricting Jews participating in various professions and heavily taxing Jewish businesses. As factories fell into bankruptcy, countless former line workers were forced into peddling or any work they could find, but were often unable to feed their families on their meager earnings.

Not surprisingly, as things worsened locally, the Zionist dream looked better and better. Ze'ev (Vladimir) Jabotinsky, the founder of the Zionist Betar youth movement, was royally welcomed in Kalisz in 1930. Indeed many locals would participate in Aliyah Bet beginning in 1933, even when entrance was clandestine, since it was heavily curtailed by the tiny quotas of Jews the British would allow into Palestine. These quotas would remain in effect until the gates swung open at Israeli statehood in 1948.

And pogroms, attacks on Jews, began to occur with greater frequency in the early '30s. A terrible instance of this violent form of scapegoating occurred one day in 1931, when Jewish peddlers set out with whatever they had to sell at the fair in nearby Grodzisk, 13 wagons worth. They were greeted with shouts of "Out with the Jews!" their merchandise was stolen and they were savagely beaten. A total of 162 Jews were injured that day including Feivsh Messer, a father of six who was stabbed in the head. Witnesses reported that their cries for help were ignored by the local police.

As the standard banks struggled to keep up with the demand for loans and withdrawals, eventually going under themselves, the Jewish community united to use whatever resources that remained to help Jews who were struggling. Called into duty were grassroots credit unions, individual charities and the Jewish community's sorely overtaxed Relief Committee. In 1932, some 70 percent of the city's Jews applied for aid to get them through Passover.

What little ability the Jews of Kalisz had to rebound from the market crash of '29 was soon crushed by the rise to power of Hitler and the Nazi party just across the border. Standing at the precipice of disaster in 1931, up to their ankles in bankrupt factories, closed schools, failing banks, anti-Semitic restrictions and hungry children were the 19,248 Jews of Kalisz, a full 35 percent of the total population.

In an essay republished in the *Kalisz Memorial Book: The History of the Jews of Kalisz* (New York Public Library and the National Yiddish Book Center, 2003), Dr. S. Zalud writes lovingly of growing up in this warm and nurturing Jewish community, one that is now forever gone. He describes the living, breathing streets with names like Babina (where my dad grew up), Nowa,

Chopin and Ciasna, the mouth-watering smells of the bakeries and butchers, the sounds of the singing that poured from the little Hasidic *shtieblech*, "the music that filled the air especially on Shabbat and holidays." He also reminisced about a certain corner of the park near the waterfall that served as meeting spot for the Zionistic young people involved in Hashomer Hatsair, where other songs – these singing of a Jewish homeland in rudimentary Hebrew -- would pierce the night air.

But there is another, less happy, memory: from the following year when, as a boy, Dr. Zalud watched a pogrom turn his usually happy, peaceful neighborhood into something dark and dangerous. "Christian youth in the streets stood menacingly holding sticks in their hands," he wrote, recalling that he and the other children were sent home from school that day. The butchers resisted, he recalls, and one paid with his life, while other Jews gathered to weep in the synagogue.

Dr. Zalud calls his essay "a dream ramble through something that once existed and has vanished ... the city stands with all its beauty and charm, but the Jews are no longer there. Their birthplace has betrayed them. It has forgotten them. But we remember. Let us hold them dear in our memory."

———

CHAPTER 4

From Anti-Semitism to Planned Destruction: 1933 to 1939

---

*"My poor people, put on sackcloth and strew dust on
yourselves! Mourn as for an only child. Wail bitterly
for suddenly the destroyer is coming upon us."*

-- JEREMIAH 6:26

1933

THE YEAR WAS 1933, KNOWN as 5693 on the Jewish calendar. The world had fallen into the depths of the Great Depression and it was the beginning of the end for European Jewry. Of course at the time no one knew how terrifying things would soon become. On January 30, Adolf Hitler had himself appointed German chancellor, setting in motion what would become the Nazi genocide against the Jews. Two months later in a heavily rigged election, Hitler was officially elected and soon thereafter his Nazi party effectively took dictatorial powers, outlawing all political parties in Germany – except his own.

What was happening in Germany in 1933 – the increasing number of new laws victimizing Jews there – was destined to have deadly repercussions over the border. In just a few years, the Germans and their anti-Semitic allies among the Poles, Ukrainians, Romanians, Croatians and other collaborators were able to destroy a strong and vibrant Jewish world. For Kalisz, it was the end of 800 years of Jewish life, beginning the day the first Jew arrived in town in 1139.

First the enemy destroyed their livelihood. Already staggering under the scarcity of the Great Depression, Jews were hit with a series of anti-Semitic laws that tightened the noose around their neck. with heavy taxation and restrictions on where and how they could earn a livelihood. And with attacks on salesmen and peddlers trying to sell what few wares they could get their hands on.

As Edith Gomolka wrote in her memoir, the anti-Semitism in Kalisz was palpable even when she was a girl. "The Jewish people lived in an oppressive and anti-Semitic society," she wrote, enumerating the restrictions on higher education (quotas allowed 2 percent of the state university classes to be made up of Jews), on business hours (Jews were not even allowed to sell to other Jews on Sundays) and jobs (no Jews for instance were permitted in the town employ). Her own aunt and uncle were attacked on the street one evening, she recounts, and her aunt's resulting head injury proved fatal.

The government was soon stripping Jews of their religious autonomy, culture and even their sense of peoplehood, by outlawing kosher slaughtering and other religious activities, and wresting power from what had been, even in the worst of times, largely a self-governed community.

And within a few short years they took from them their very lives – between 1939 and 1945, more than 90 percent of Poland's 3.5 million Jews were murdered by the Germans and their henchmen. That statistic never fails to remind me both of the enormity of the crime and what a miracle it was that both my parents were able to get out of there alive.

But in 1933 the Jewish community was increasingly shaken by what they were hearing from their cousins and friends just across the border. In Germany the year saw the enforcement of the Nuremberg Laws which stole most of that country's Jews' rights, and broadened the definition of who is a Jew to include anyone who had at least three Jewish grandparents. This was true even if they were not considered Jewish by Jewish law and even if they did not dress, worship or live traditionally. It became suddenly clear that a secular Jew teaching at a university in Berlin and long assimilated into German society was no safer than his traditional cousin learning Talmud in a *shtetl* -- a small Jewish village – far removed from big city ways.

In April, Polish Jews tried to resist by forming the Committee for Fighting Persecution of Jews in Germany, declaring a boycott of German goods and welcoming the refugees pouring in from Germany as best they could in their economically depressed state.

But in Kalisz, the Jews couldn't pretend the infestation had not arrived in Poland too. The city was by then a hotbed for the publication and distribution of anti-Semitic newspapers which circulated widely through town, whipping the rest of the citizenry into an anti-Semitic fever.

These publications often featured cartoons stereotyping "dirty Jews" dressed in traditional Orthodox garb. And the vicious portrayals of the Jews filling these pages also frequently included allegations of blood libel. Much of this anti-Semitic propaganda came from the local Endecja party which had been behind many attacks on Jews over the years and an ongoing campaign to enforce a boycott on Jewish businessmen and artisans.

In addition, Jewish peddlers and salesmen were increasingly beaten in the '30s especially if they ventured outside their own neighborhood. I remember my mother telling me how she and her mother begged her father, my grandfather Yitzhak who'd often traveled to sell his leather wares, not to risk the trip since so many businessmen in their town of Radom, Poland were being attacked. My grandmother Tirtza also pleaded with my

Chopping off Jewish men's beards was a widespread sport by the Nazis and their supporters even before the war began

grandfather to shave off his beard since the Poles had been grabbing Jewish men by their beards and cutting them off, often injuring the man in the process. I am not sure if he curtailed his business travel. But, though I will never know for sure, I have every reason to believe that my grandfather died with his beard intact -- most likely in Treblinka in August, 1942 with the 20,000 other Jews taken during the second major "liquidation" of the Radom ghetto.

And these hardships also wreaked havoc on the Jewish community itself. The teachers at the Talmud Torah, who had 400 children in their care, had not received salaries for some time. Their families starving, eventually they broke with tradition and went on strike. When the Kehilla scraped together some funds to pay them, the teachers returned to their classrooms.

Not surprisingly, as many as who could get away to Palestine, even during the British attempts to cut off this immigration, did so in a movement known as Aliyah Bet which saw 174,000 Jews mostly from Eastern Europe flooding in. Called *Hashgama* in Hebrew, this movement attracted many of the young people who grew up in the Hashomer Hatsair, a movement that in this case would save their lives. Included among them: My great uncle Abraham Wolkovitch whom, as you may recall, convinced my grandfather Mayer to follow him. Which he did until he was brutally attacked and took to heart the Arabs' warning to return to Poland.

1934

The Yiddish weekly *Kaliszer Leben* (*Kalisz Life*) welcomed 1934 with a thin ray of hope. "We part sadly from the (year) that is departing, bearing with it the whole weight of worries and concern." But 1934 was destined to see more and more Jews slipping deeper and deeper into poverty and needing aid simply to survive.

Because so many Jewish children were going to bed hungry each night, the community supported a summer camp. The *Kaliszer Leben* proudly reported that the campers gained an average of 3 kilo (over 6 pounds) after a summer of eating regular healthful meals and playing in the fresh air.

On the world scene, it was a dangerous time as war clouds began to gather over Europe. The German–Polish Non-Aggression Pact, an international treaty between Nazi Germany and the Second Polish Republic, was signed and sealed in the early weeks of that winter. The bottom line: Germany and Poland promised to avoid any military confrontation with each other for 10 full years. Of course, the 20/20 hindsight that history gives us reminds us that the German army would invade Poland a mere five years later.

1935

Kaliszer Leben would sum up 1935 in a few choice words: "chaos … an unbearable economic crisis." The numbers tell the tale: Since the worldwide market crashed in late 1929, things had worsened considerably as Christian business owners grabbed the Jews' share of a limited market by convincing the city's leaders to enact new restrictions and taxes on their Jewish competitors. Between 1932 to 1935, the average income of a Kalisz Jew fell by another 30 percent.

In addition, after 1935, anti-Semitic political parties in Poland turned up pressure on the government to restrict where and how Jews lived. Emboldened by the new anti-Semitic laws in Nazi Germany, these politicos saw no reason why Poles could not follow suit, eliminating one by one the professional and personal freedoms of the Jews.

But Jews by tradition tend to revert to hope and typically refuse to surrender until they find a way to fight back against oppression, whatever the source. One bright spot during this difficult time: the community mustered its strength to celebrate the completion of writing a new Torah scroll. (You have to wonder what's become of it).

In that spirit, even in these ever-darkening times, the city's Jewish cooperative credit unions did whatever they could to keep businesses from going under. This in the face of a greatly worsened business climate, escalating right up until the German invasion in the fall of 1939.

Other self-help efforts included the founding of a new local chapter of ORT, training unemployed Jews and also arranging for low interest loans. And the Small Merchants Society continued to advocate for their members who were by now barred from the local fairs and markets where they had for centuries been able to sell their wares to the general populace.

But things had gotten so bad by this time that my father could see that the dwindling revenues from his father's small lace factory could no longer support the three of them. At age 25, my dad knew that if he were going to make a future for himself, it would not be in economically depressed Kalisz with the Nazis in nearby Germany literally breathing down the city's neck. So he left home, making his way to Bydgoszcz where he worked as a sales rep for a sweater manufacturer, eventually moving up to the larger territory of Poznan.

1936

Meanwhile, back at home, the formerly dominant Agudat party was struggling to keep up its leadership role among the Jews of Kalisz. Their condition was worsening, described by the usually optimistic *Kaliszer Leben* as "difficult and bitter ... a year of harsh experiences and sad developments, economic decrees, anti-Semitic incitement, unbridled as it was, and the acute economic boycott."

Indeed those editors were not blind to the phenomenon affecting all of Polish Jewry, some 3.5 million men, women and children, be they sophisticated city dwellers, traditional shtetl Jews or backwoods farmers. The times, they wrote had "given rise to a mood of despair and helplessness," fueled by bloody pogroms and a growing list of new and punishing laws and economic restrictions.

An example: in August 1936, the Polish government began requiring the name of the owner must be clearly marked on the front of each store. Meaning that everyone was to know which were Jewish-owned businesses. Not surprisingly, the number Jewish stores and other businesses attacked and looted increased dramatically as soon as this order took effect.

As more and more businesses closed their doors, demands on the Gemelut Chassidim Society, the Linat Hatsedek Society and other relief organizations increased as the Jewish community rallied to help out their brethren as much as possible with food, shelter, medicine and other necessities.

Though it would still be three years before they invaded Poland, by this time the Nazis found Kalisz, perched just on the other side of the Polish-German border, to be fertile territory for their anti-Semitism. Based on its unfortunate location, it is not surprising that the city was destined to be among the Nazis' earliest conquests, their focus on torturing Jews after the September, 1939 invasion made all the easier by the years of anti-Semitic indoctrination leading up to it.

At this time there were 26,000 Jews in the city, nearly double the 1914 figure. The town saw an escalation of virulent anti-Semitic press then as well as increasing violence against those few stalwart peddlers still trying to sell at local fairs and the central market of Poznan. As the newspaper reported, "the Poles rob them of their goods and beat them murderously."

The situation – attacks both in the street and in the press – resulted in a trip to Warsaw by leaders of the local Jewish community to meet with the Minister of Interior, General Felicjan Slawoj-Skladkowski. The general pledged that the Jews would be allowed to sell at the local fairs and markets, safely. But if any good that came out of the meeting, the benefit was soon lost in the increasing – and often legally sanctioned -- assaults over the next few years.

On a personal note, one of the general stores my father sold goods to in Radom, Poland at this time was owned by my maternal grandfather Yitzhak Freidenreich (Like my other grandparents, he would be killed by the Nazis a decade before I was born so I would never have a chance to meet any of them).

Dad recalls often checking into a Jewish hotel called the Mentlik. By the way, the hotel's sign at Ulica Wałowa 1 in current-day Radom, with its original Yiddish inscription, is still there, one of the very few visible remnants of that once-thriving Jewish community.

This weathered sign for the Mentlik Hotel, where my dad often stayed on his Radom sales trips, is one of the few signs left of Jewish life in that city

By the way, here's a picture of me at 61 Zeromskiego Street in the center of Radom, where my maternal grandfather's original general store had been a landmark for decades – my mother and her two sisters and brother grew up in the apartment in back of the store. That lasted until the Freidenreich family was sent to the ghetto with the rest of the Jews of Radom. The meager corner rations shop they ran there – a far cry from my grandfather Yitzhak's upscale store downtown -- was where my parents first met.

My mom and her siblings grew up here in her family's store where my father would make sales calls.

My parents both recall that initial sighting in 1940, after Mom's family were moved to the ghetto, a time when life had changed dramatically for the Jews and they were living in greatly reduced quarters and on barely subsistence food. My dad being

12 years my mom's senior (29 vs. 17 at the time), to this teenaged girl he seemed like an older man -- albeit a very nice looking one, she recalls to this day.

It was around this time that my dad got to be friendly with my mother's older cousins from the Moshovitz family – her mother's sister Chava's children – especially sisters Nuta and Carola, who both survived the war along with brothers Marcel, Mark and Jerry. This was quite remarkable considering the statistical odds against all these siblings living through those deadly years.

1937

On the very first day of the year, a law was passed that placed further limits on kosher slaughtering and sale of kosher meat. So severe was this law that the government effectively reduced the ability to supply kosher meat to only 3 percent of the total Jewish population, most of whom only ate meat slaughtered in the time-honored way of the Torah and their forefathers. It also had a devastating effect on the income of thousands of families who made their living raising and slaughtering the animals and selling the meat.

Other laws that pushed the Jewish community into untenable situations were introduced this year, including shopkeepers only permitted to sell their wares in a small area of the town market, a placement strictly enforced by Polish nationalist guards. The law was effective in its intent: preventing Christians from shopping at Jewish-owned stalls.

Other laws enacted in 1937 included a ban on Jewish doctors -- the Polish Medical Association now effectively barred them from practicing. And similarly the Polish Bar Association soon forbade Jews from practicing law, followed the next year with a rule that no Jew could be granted a license to practice law anywhere in Poland.

Around this time, there was discussion between the French and Polish government about the possibility of sending thousands of their Jews to Madagascar to live. A commission was dispatched to the island, at the time a French territory, to assess the situation. The plan was shelved after they discovered that, not only would the cost of shipping the Jews over be high, but no more than a few thousand could fit, a small dent in the 3 million Jews they were trying to rid themselves of.

1938

This year, even more professions began barring Jews from participating. In January it was the General Assembly of Journalists in Vilna that included in its by-laws a no-Jewish-member proviso. And three months later, the Bank Polski (Polish Bank), Poland's biggest financial institution, also added a rule banning Jews from working there.

By 1938 my dad was back in Kalisz pretty much full-time since, with his friend Joseph Rockman, he opened a textile store selling men's suiting fabric. But he continued to travel around much of the country on selling trips.

So, unlike many Polish Jews who only knew the hard times impacting their own cities or towns, my dad witnessed many of the terrible happenings in big cities like Warsaw as well as smaller ones like Radom. That meant that, when he would visit another city on business or return home, he would bring with him the news of the rest of the country. And, though by nature an optimist, my father was also a realist and, knowing him, I suspect he told it the way he saw it.

This year, the screws tightened even further on what was left of Kalisz's kosher meat market, virtually cutting off the supply. The city had been re-assigned to the Poznan district, an area where kosher slaughtering was strictly prohibited. Even after intensive lobbying of the powers-that-be, the local slaughterers were permitted to produce only a small amount of kosher meat, which supplied only a few families and left most Jews with no way to get kosher meat.

This was also the year that Poland adopted a new "Citizenship Law." Designed to keep many thousands of Jews from coming home, it revoked the passports of Poles who'd been out of the country for five years or longer. This meant that Polish Jews who had been living in Germany were now trapped there.

This could not have come at a worse time for these Jews as, over the border in Germany, the Nazis were pledging to throw Polish Jews out of the country. So the Jews were effectively trapped between the two countries. In October, 15,000 Polish Jews were turned back by Polish border guards and then sent to the sub-human conditions in a refugee camp in Zbaszyn. This was an early and foreboding sign of the Germans' "final solution" and an indication that they had every intention of catching Poland's 3.5 million Jews in its murderous net.

Polish Jews, especially those as close at hand as the Kaliszers, were also keenly aware of what happened in Germany on November 9, a terrifying experience that history now knows as Kristallnacht, the Night of the Broken Glass. Over the period of a few short hours, the Nazis and their henchmen systematically destroyed – mostly by fire -- more than 900 synagogues. They also broke into and looted homes, businesses and schools in Jewish neighborhoods, threw 30,000 Jews in jail and killed nearly 100 others.

Also in November, Herschel Grynszpan, a 17-year-old Polish Jew living in Paris, shot Ernst vom Rath, a German diplomat living in Paris. Although Grynszpan apparently was incensed that his parents, along with countless other Polish Jews had been taken from their homes, the Nazis claimed the shooting was a Jewish plot.

Following Kristallnacht, the Germans were far from apologetic. They levied a fine of $400 million on the Jewish community in Germany, and forced Jews to clean up the wreckage. They also diverted any insurance money paid out for damages into their own coffers.

The lesson of Kristallnacht was duly noted by those like-minded leaders in Poland who were watching and waiting their turn to destroy Jewish life in their country too and ultimately the Jews themselves. Less than 10 months later, as the German army marched into Kalisz on September 4, 1939, they would have their chance. Like the rest of Polish Jewry, nine out of 10 of Kalisz's 27,000 Jews' days were numbered.

———

CHAPTER 5

The Final Years: The Holocaust

―――――

"The waters from the sea will dry up, And the river will
be parched and dry. The canals will emit a stench. The
streams of Egypt will thin out and dry up; The reeds
and rushes will rot away. The bulrushes by the Nile, by
the edge of the Nile and all the sown fields by the Nile
will become dry, be driven away, and be no more."

-- ISAIAH 19:5-8

AT THE DAWN OF 1939 Kalisz, perched so close to the Polish-German border, was home to more than 27,000 Jews, roughly a third of the city's population and nearly double the 1914 figure. But, as we've learned in the previous chapter, by then the city's Jews were already living highly constrained lives. Restricted to where they could live and do business and barred from an increasing number of professions, most Jews struggled every day to feed their families. Now, with anti-Semitic propaganda circulating throughout the region, and the city having declared a boycott of all Jewish merchants and stores, the noose was tightening on Kalisz's Jews.

By then, the Nazis, encouraged and abetted by the Endecja party and other homegrown anti-Semites, including many in the local media, found in Kalisz many ideological allies, even before they arrived in force.

1939, THE NAZI INVASION AND BEYOND

On September 4, 1939 the German army marched into town and the city, mounting little in the way of self-defense, was officially absorbed into the Reich territory, a region which would be officially renamed a few months later as Warthegau.

Only a year after the invasion, only 1,000 Kalisz Jews remained and, though some escaped, historians agree that the vast majority of the 27,000 Jews who lived in Kalisz a short year earlier were no longer among the living.

Of course, not only was this the end for them as individuals and as family trees with their branches sawed off, but also for the Jewish community of Kalisz. For much of precisely 800 years -- 1139 until 1939 – roughly a third of the city had been Jewish, a community that had flourished and exerted a substantial influence on both the local culture and the city's economic infrastructure.

You know the old riddle: What's the difference between a Jewish pessimist and a Jewish optimist? A Jewish pessimist says things can't possibly be any worse than they are right now. A Jewish optimist says, "Yes they can!" For the Jews who must not have thought things could get worse, after September 4, 1939, they suddenly did. The Germans began tormenting them as soon as they marched into the city. And the Jews had no defense for their homes, businesses or synagogues, much less their personal safety and that of their children. Those who appeared able-bodied were snatched off the streets and sent off to slave labor camps, a curfew was declared, homes and businesses were seized – the few remaining stores had to post a sign declaring "Jude" – and as elsewhere across occupied Poland, Jewish students were no longer permitted to attend schools. I remember my mom telling me that she was heartbroken to be told she couldn't come back to her beloved school, and so bored that she took up crocheting just to have something to occupy her when she was tending her father's small shop in the Radom ghetto.

In addition, not only were the streets all given German names but a sign went up that read "Kalisz Without Jews." On the heels of the invasion, the Jews marked Rosh Hashanah and the rest of the high holidays as best they could, but already the scarcity of food and demands for all able-bodied Jews over 13 to work for the invaders made celebrating difficult at best. Synagogues and study houses were closed, anything silver stolen from them and Torah scrolls burned in the street while in many neighborhoods young Jewish girls were forced to dance around the flames.

Indeed torturing Jews emerged as a leading form of entertainment for many of the invading soldiers. There were multiple reports of German soldiers commanding Jews to hold prayer services in the street, to sing and dance. Elderly men were ordered to punch each other for the soldiers' amusement. And Wehrmacht troops never tired of their favorite "sport" – chopping off religious men's beards and *payos* (earlocks), often with skin still attached. Women were also taken as maids in the houses that the Germans had commandeered and countless women and girls were violated sexually as well. They were often ordered to undress and raped and then left for dead, while their brothers continued to be taken for burying the dead and other menial jobs.

By October, there was also a slew of new regulations – against kosher slaughtering, for instance -- with the mayor himself outlawing the buying or selling of Jewish businesses. In addition, the cantor of the Reform synagogue was told to organize a Judenrat, a council of 25 of the leading Jews – businessmen, doctors, lawyers, bankers and engineers -- designated to be the conduit of Nazi orders to the city's Jewish community.

The first order of business for the Judenrat was conducting a detailed census listing every Jew in town, their professions, the number and ages of their children and a complete inventory of their possessions, from real estate to jewelry to home furnishings and even their clothing. Once supplied with this information, the Nazis began to charge the Jews for "war compensation" on all their assets, a tax that increased as the war continued. Within weeks, the Jews – some 18,000 remaining of the original 27,000 (a third had fled, been taken for labor or killed) – were now required to supply a steady stream of property and cash as well as workers as demanded by the Nazis. Soon all property was commanded to be turned over and the wealthy's attempts to hide their assets were routinely discovered and the goods confiscated, often under the guise of surprise house-to-house weapon searches.

But frequently it was difficult for the Germans to tell who was Jewish. "So they needed to use 'favorable assistants' as they were called, or collaborators," Gomolka recalls. "Their work was to verify the religious heritage of an individual. The Germans started dragging in Jews from the streets and then from their homes and forced them with terror to perform slave labor," she added. "This behavior was called 'Aktion.'"

In order to fulfill this order, the Judenrat was forced to tax those in the community who still had property of any kind and order 150-400 workers daily to report for duty to do whatever the Nazis needed done. The richer Jews could be relieved of the latter duty by paying 2 zloty a day. Workers were not paid and were often beaten, but sometimes received a meager serving of soup and bread during the work day.

The Nazis had also done their homework about this close-by city they were invading. One of their first orders of business when they took power was pulling out many of the embroidery and lace-making machines from the Jewish factories and transporting them to Germany to support the war effort.

Of course, the Jews harbored dreams of escape. In Kalisz, as noted above, thousands of Jews fled from the city in the first month of German rule, many risking being shot to cross over the Russian border to an uncertain future. Indeed, of those who succeeded in getting over the border alive, many would find Russia to be less than hospitable and were doomed to be killed in the forests there or in the camps. In some Russian towns and villages as in Poland and Germany, in the early days of the war before the Germans had established their concentration camps, the Jews were often told to report to the local Jewish cemetery where they would be ordered to dig their own graves and shot by firing squads. In other instances, these mass murders occurred in a forested area on the outskirts of town. Decades later, many eye witnesses were able to lead authorities to the site of these mass graves. But until today, most of these mass graves are still unknown and lack any marker indicating whose final resting place they are.

Of those attempting escape, there were countless families who traveled by wagon or on foot with very little idea of where they could be safe and equally little in the way of food and other supplies. Plenty of them headed for relatives' homes in rural areas. "Many people thought the smaller villages would be free from danger," Gomolka wrote. "They thought small towns being small targets were of little strategic importance and they would be spared the hardship of the ensuing war."

Thousands of Polish Jews ran to Romania, Hungary and Lithuania, while still others, in a desperate attempt to reach Palestine, crowded aboard ships in ports in Bulgaria and Romania. But in Turkey, where they needed to refuel, the powers-that-be refused to allow many of the desperate refugees access to Palestine since, as we've seen, the Brits' White Paper permitted very few Jews into the country during these years.

Many a Polish Jew, finding all escape routes barred to them, gave up after weeks or months on the road, turned around and headed home. But those who fled to Lodz and Warsaw tended not to return to hometowns like Kalisz but were more often swept away in the equally horrible fate awaiting the Jews in these two larger cities.

Descriptions of Kalisz's Jewish neighborhood a mere month into German rule by resident Wolf Lassman depict a landscape of looted and empty stores – the nights filled with the sound of gunshots and the mornings with the sight of bodies left in the street, "like a city of the dead."

For the young and the fit, or those with specialized skills, the only hope for staying alive was providing the labor that the Germans needed to sustain both the war effort and the killing of the Jews and others they also considered unfit to live, including the disabled, socialists and homosexuals. In Kalisz, because of its history, this work often involved textiles, including uniforms and dress clothes, hats and even fur coats for the officers and their families. And, in a town also known for its leather work (something my mother's family in Radom traded in), Jewish workers provided belts and shoes for the Nazis. The

Jews were also put to work making the wooden shoes that would be part of the regulation concentration camp uniform for the next six years.

During that autumn additional new restrictions on Kalisz's Jews came fast and furious. By October, Jewish mill owners were forbidden to buy grain and were limited in how much flour they could produce, plus the number of Jewish bakers permitted to work in the city dropped to three. That month the Jews had to transfer any foreign currencies they still owned to German credit banks and both the Poles and the Jews of Kalisz were forced to surrender their radios to the police.

"We were now a part of Germany ... and were designated to become "Jude Rein" which meant cleansed of all Jews," Gomolka writes. "This was part of a plan by the Germans to make way for the growing German population and use the Jews as a scapegoat for everyone's problems."

November brought even more stringent crack-downs. A curfew was instituted after 5 each evening, staying in effect until 8 the next morning. More Torah scrolls were burned and German soldiers destroyed the city's Great Synagogue where, 16 years earlier, my father joined the generations of young Kalisz boys who celebrated their bar mitzvahs in that stately old building. As best as can be determined, this was when the tributary was stopped up with the stones, furnishings, prayer books and other religious objects from that synagogue and other Jewish buildings, plus books from local public libraries, never to flow again.

And that also was the month that all local Jews – from babies to the elderly -- were now required to wear a yellow Jewish star band printed with "Jude" on their right arm and chest, and were forbidden to travel beyond a proscribed area.

**Anyone Jewish found without the required yellow
Jewish star was subject to immediate murder**

In November, some 10,000 of Kalisz Jews were thrown out of
their homes which were then occupied by German officers and
their supporters from both Poland and the Baltics. Instructed to
bring their linens and meet in Market Square, the men, women
and children were whipped with rubber truncheons and herded
into a warehouse and many of the more well-to-do were cross
examined as to where their valuables were hidden. Within two
weeks they were shipped off to the Lodz ghetto and from there,
most were eventually sent to the death camps.

Incredibly, the Nazis did not stop at having the Jews locked
up within a small area; they demanded they pay for their own

food, security, sewage removal and the other expenses incurred by their continuing incarceration.

It soon became clear that what the Germans really had in mind was to "cleanse" not only their own country but their newly acquired Poland of all Jews. Even before the network of concentration camps was erected, Jews were being deported into ghettos in major cities or forced to dig mass graves and then gunned down in the woods surrounding their hometowns. In fact by early 1940, almost all of Kalisz's Jews who were still alive had been deported to the Jewish ghettos in Warsaw, Lodz or Lublin.

The Lodz Ghetto, second in size only to Warsaw, was known for its extreme hardships and was a common stop enroute to the deathcamps for Kalisz Jews

November was also the month when the fate of the town's remaining Jews was determined. The Judenrat was informed that a ghetto would also be established in Kalisz, which turned out to be a falsehood designed to flush out the remaining Jews living beyond the mythical ghetto's borders.

Survivors reported that they were given 10 minutes to pack and limited to 15 kg (33 pounds) per person. Some were temporarily crowded into the Observant monastery. And on November 20, the Germans pushed still more Kalisz Jews into a trade hall with little in the way of sanitation. After being searched and any money and valuables confiscated, they were locked in and for several days lived without food. The Germans also sent in to join them all surviving members of the Judenrat.

More than three weeks passed before many of the Jews in the trade hall were sent by train to ghettos near Lublin and Podlachia and from there to the death camps in Belz or Sobibór. Others were dispatched to labor camps. But, being December, many died in the unheated cattle vans from frostbite and starvation well before reaching their destinations.

By the end of the year, some 6,800 men, women and children Jews – nearly a quarter of Kalisz Jews – had found their way to the Warsaw ghetto, most of them destined to be killed there or in the gas chambers of Treblinka and Birkenau.

Indeed, by all reports, by the end of 1939 nearly every Jew had been deported except for a handful of workers and the Jewish Hospital's patients and staff. During these early months the Germans and their henchmen stole anything of value belonging to the city's 27,000-plus Jews, and there were reports that many of the Polish young women asked for – and received -- much of the jewelry that had belonged to the Jewish women.

Alas, my father's family was not immune to the terrorizing of Kalisz Jews. In the autumn of 1939, when the Germans marched into Poland, my dad was a month shy of his 29th birthday and still traveling and selling fabrics for men's suits.

That fall was the last time my father would see his parents. Baylah and Mayer Kempner were in a group taken to the Lodz ghetto that fall and then to the Chelmno concentration camp in 1941 where it seems likely they were gassed soon after they arrived. Were they too old to appear useful to the Nazis? Did they lack the skills that could have saved their lives, at least for a while? We will never know. All we know is that their names are included on the German's list of those shipped from the Lodz ghetto to Chelmno, which was a death sentence for nearly everyone.

Chelmno: A death camp that was the end of the road for many Kalisz Jews, including my Kempner grandparents

By the time my grandparents, along with thousands of other Kalisz Jews, were taken, my adventuresome father was no longer in Kalisz. Hearing that Zwolen hadn't been taken over by Nazis yet, he relocated there. But after some Poles held a resistance rally where they had burned a picture of Hitler in the town square, suddenly Zwolen was anything but safe to remain in. The Germans began to bomb the city and my dad made his way on foot and hitchhiking to Radom. When he arrived, he discovered that many of his friends (including some of my mom's cousins) had escaped to the Lodz ghetto.

Once back in Radom, my father remembers meeting a prominent Jewish businessman from Lodz who had represented a large textile manufacturer prior to the war. This fellow liked my father and introduced him to other key Jewish business contacts living in Radom who had access to rare apartments, permits and merchandise. Among them was a Mrs. Reichman who had been in the gold jewelry business back in Lodz.

My father told us all about how he agreed to help this Mrs. Reichman smuggle the remaining gold she had out of the Warsaw ghetto to sell on the black market. He had already earned a name for himself as a skilled black marketer by selling, buying and transporting contraband goods between the Warsaw and Radom ghettos, a highly risky business in occupied Poland.

But unfortunately, my dad's luck in transporting contraband was about to run out.

Having convinced a doctor friend of his to use his more liberal medical travel permit to help get textile piece goods out of the Lodz ghetto, my dad had a plan: to smuggle the goods into Radom to sell to clothing manufacturers.

The two men had executed their plan of traveling to Lodz, buying the textiles and then hiding them in a horse drawn wagon. So far so good. But on the road back to Radom their wagon was stopped and searched by a unit of German soldiers.

The Nazis found and confiscated the piece goods, tore up the doctor's medical travel permit and verbally and physically abused both men.

My dad and his doctor friend returned to Radom bruised and shaken and with empty pockets but relieved to have escaped with their lives. And soon, like many other Polish Jews, the doctor took off for the Russian border, reasoning he was better off there than in Poland. It was a gambit that paid off for some but would end tragically for others, sadly including the doctor.

In November my dad was captured in Radom and sent to the ghetto there. By the spring of 1941, like many other Jews, he was relocated to the Warsaw ghetto, the next step in an incredible odyssey which would eventually lead him into an even more incredible new life.

1940

Among the largest of the ghettos the Nazis had formed to warehouse the Jews were Warsaw and Lodz, and those absorbed many thousands of Kalisz Jews. Opened in February of 1940, the Lodz ghetto would pack them in at a density averaging 3.5 people in a single room – effectively cutting them off from the rest of the world.

By Passover, 1940 any Jew from infants to old *bubbes* (Yiddish for grandmothers) caught without the yellow star with 'Jude' in mock Hebraic print on both the shoulder and chest would be arrested. Lest you assume all of this was the work of the German army alone, however, history says otherwise; much of it was carried out and enforced by the Jews' old neighbors, the Poles.

But there was a smattering of Polish Jews who, even as the Nazi net drew tighter around Eastern European Jewry, managed to escape. Some 15,000 fled to Lithuania and 2,000 made it via Vladivostok to ships bound for Japan. This was made possible due to an unlikely alliance between Dutch and Japanese officials.

Other escapees were less fortunate. The Turks refused to permit entrance into Palestine so that, in the winter of 1942, the ship "Struma" sank off the coast of Turkey when its 769 Jewish refugees attempting to reach Palestine were refused docking in Istanbul. The ship was towed into the Black Sea where it was torpedoed by the Soviets. There was only one known survivor.

Another tragic escape was that of the 7,000 Kalisz Jews who made it out to the Warsaw ghetto, most of them doomed to die in the bombings and other brutal attacks that transpired there. Some 1,300 of the strongest Jews were taken to a local slave labor camp and many of these were forced to use the gravestones from the Jewish cemetery in building projects for the German army.

All of this movement left fewer than 700 Jews in Kalisz by summer's end and, in October of that year, many of them were judged "unfit" and taken into the forest where they were shot. Others were moved into factories on Ul. Złota (Golden Street). Those few survivors were put to work in manufacturing clothing and shoes as well as maintenance functions.

This was the year the hospital patients would be "transferred for convalescence." When the large black truck arrived in late October, at first the patients did not realize it was in fact a mobile killing machine equipped with lethal gas. The truck made several trips over two days killing hundreds of the sick and infirm. Ironically, the Council of Elders was charged for each of these people to be "transported," victims who were instead gassed and then buried in the forests surrounding Kalisz.

These mobile killing machines were soon abandoned as too slow and inefficient and the Germans with their Polish helpers were busy constructing the large killing camps, including Auschwitz and Treblinka. But until this system was completed, the majority of the Jews of Poland were forced into ghettos which functioned as holding tanks. Once "relocated" there, they could not leave (except those few on official business). In the ghettos many were starved, beaten, shot or worked to death. Still others were rounded up in groups and taken to isolated fields and forests outside of town where they were forced to dig huge graves before being mowed down by gunfire. The rare Jew who survived and other witnesses would eventually be able to testify to these mass killings but, as noted above, many of these mass graves remain undiscovered to this day.

Remember the Madagascar Plan? In 1940 the Nazis resurrected this plan that the French and Polish governments had been considering back in 1937. The idea: Moving as many of their Jews to the island of Madagascar, which was at the time a French colony (The Germans it appears were not the only anti-Semitic government in Europe at the time). Though the French and Poles had scrapped the plan as being too expensive and not having enough capacity for the number of Jews they hoped to rid themselves of, the Germans resuscitated the idea of shipping the Jews there – Hitler himself was a proponent of it. Their idea: Let the money and goods they were stealing from German and Polish Jews finance the move. But the idea was once again shelved, due both to its projected cost and the defeat of the Germans in the Battle of Britain.

Instead, the Nazis had already conceived of and were well on their way to executing their "final solution," the wholesale murder of Europe's Jews, initially by gunfire either in – or at the outskirts of -- their hometowns and later in the ghettos the Nazis created as holding cells and in the death camps they would soon be building mostly in Poland. Many others died of illness or starvation in the ghettos and camps, still others were worked mercilessly until they dropped dead of exhaustion.

1941

Though only some 400 Jews remained in the city, in 1941, a ghetto actually was created in Kalisz, which remained in force until the summer of 1942. The Jews there were mostly workers in shoemaking and tailoring for the Nazi army. By the end of 1941, however, nearly half of them had been sent to die at Chelmno and nearly all the rest had been shipped off to the Lodz ghetto and from there likewise ending up in Chelmno where they were also killed.

Just like my grandparents, my father's parents Mayer and Baylah whose names are clearly recorded on a document it is hard to argue with (the Germans' own list of Jews in the Lodz ghetto), the vast majority of them – some 70,000 men, women and children -- were transferred to Chelmno death camp throughout 1941 and 1942; the others were rounded up a few months later and taken to the Lodz Jewish cemetery where they were gunned down. The US Holocaust Memorial has this and many other such lists on file which, as terrible as it is to accept, at least put an end to families' false hopes that their loved ones survived.

But though my grandparents perished like the great majority of Kalisz Jews, their son lived on and, because he did, my sister and I are here today, and so are my three grown kids and

11 grandchildren. Since the odds of my parents' survival was so small, each one of us is a miracle.

But it was a circuitous and difficult path to survival for my father. Captured on November 28, 1939 most likely while trying to make another smuggling run into the Radom ghetto, he remained there until he was sent to the Warsaw ghetto in the spring of 1941, then to the Kielce ghetto in December of that year. And, because he was healthy and strong, from there he was sent to the work camp at Kielce in September of 1942 and from there to the one in Blizyn in the spring of 1943.

There, although the work was back-breaking and he suffered a broken leg, his servitude also had an outcome that would prove pretty good for my sister and me: It was in Blizyn that he met our mother again. He told her then that, if they both somehow managed to survive, he would find her. It was a promise he would keep, against all odds, three years later, after he was liberated from Mauthausen concentration camp on May 5, 1945. Another fortunate day for us all.

The few Kalisz-born Jews who, like my dad, survived, were mostly young people who could serve the Nazis in some capacity -- older people and children had much shorter life expectancies. (The story of how my mother's sewing talent saved her life again and again is recorded in *Always Good with A Needle: My Journey from Radom to Redemption*, which Deborah Fineblum also helped me write).

Even when they were driven with inhuman production quotas for 18 hours a day, survivors reported they were given only two pieces of bread and two mouthfuls of water. Other days they might subsist on a slice of bread, a bowl of soup and a cup of sour grain beverage. They were also fed a steady stream of taunts, insults and lashings with damp rubber whips when any of them appeared to slow their efforts or in some other way annoy the Germans or their henchmen. Survivors say that watching their peers be shot at rollcall or disappear into the ovens, their remains often destined for the soap factory, kept even the sickest and most exhausted inmates pushing themselves well beyond human capacity.

And, though he didn't speak much of those terrible times, my father did tell us years later that every day in Mauthausen a number of prisoners who were judged to be too weak to keep working were selected during morning rollcall, never to be seen again. These casualties were in addition to those who died overnight from illness, starvation and exhaustion.

Back in Kalisz that winter, for the few hundred remaining, the same message was clear: Work faster or die. But, as fast and hard as they worked, many fell to starvation, illness and abuse. In November, more black trucks packing deadly gas pulled into town, the end of the line for whomever was left of the older generation.

Also taken then were many of the young men who'd until then been kept alive to work. Several had decided now to fight back with anything they could get their hands on, so they don't get "led away like sheep to the slaughter," wrote survivor Dr. Moshe Gross. The Hasidim seemed at peace with their fate, he added. Many of them dressed in makeshift shrouds to be taken away – "to die consecrating HaShem's name."

Remember my dad's doctor friend who fled to Russia after the two of them were found with the black market goods? In June of 1941 the Nazis attacked Russia too. Many of the Jews in Russia were eventually sent to forced labor, or shot and shoved into mass graves outside their towns (sometimes in the Jewish cemetery) or transferred to perish in concentration camps. Sadly, the doctor was among those killed.

Then on December 1, soldiers rounded up all the remaining families with children under 12 and loaded them onto the trucks. None are known to have survived that trip. And if a baby cried, there was no pity; he or she was immediately shot.

Six days later, the Japanese bombed Pearl Harbor and two days after that, on December 9, the US declared war on Japan. Within days, on Dec 11, Hitler would declare war on the US without consulting his generals.

All of a sudden America the sleeping giant awoke from its slumber, bringing its considerable moral, personnel and industrial power to the war effort. The result: a shoring up of the Allies' beleaguered forces and a new hope of liberation to occupied Europe and what remained of its persecuted Jewish community.

1942

Early in May 1942, the Kalisz ghetto held no more than 150 Jews, warehoused in two buildings: 13 and 16 Pow Street, most of them still producing clothes and shoes. But even that small number was either deported to the Lodz ghetto (from where it was a quick trip to Chelmno) or murdered there in town by December. A handful managed to escape into the forest, often with the help of Polish friends.

So by the end of 1942, over the course of three terrifying years since the Germans rolled into town in September of 1939,

Kalisz had gone from being one-third Jewish to being officially *judenrein* (free of Jews).

1943

This was the year my dad was sent to Blizyn labor camp near Lublin, a sub-camp of Majdanek where his thigh bone was broken when, during hard labor breaking huge rock formations in a quarry, he slipped in the mud and fell hard under the tremendous weight of a boulder. After three months in a cast, he was sent to Gunskirchen, a sub-camp of Mathausen. At this point in the war the Nazis were clearly losing and making every effort to starve and work the remaining Jews to death. And my father was no exception.

But, as mentioned above, there was one bright spot for my dad at Blizyn. It was there that he and my mother met for the first time since the day she opened the door of her father's small shop in the Radom ghetto where he'd come to pick up a letter. (It was most likely from his friend – and my mother's cousin – Nuta, warning him that the Nazis were onto his smuggling activities and to lay low for a while).

My mother was at Blizyn working in the uniform factory -- she was a talented seamstress and hat maker, a skill that saved her life many times during the Shoah. And she recognized my dad. But the man who stood before her in prison garb, my mother still recalls, was a far cry from the dapperly dressed salesman she'd met at her father's small ghetto shop just two years earlier. And she had also been forced to mature quickly from the teenager she had been then.

When my father asked about her family, my mother told him that her parents and brother David had been murdered but her older sisters (also talented seamstresses) remained alive and were making dresses for the Nazis' wives and girlfriends back in Radom. So when she was offered a spot in a factory in Radom to repair artillery baskets, my mother jumped at the chance to get back to her hometown -- and her sisters, brother-in-law and little niece.

At that time my father warned her not to go back to Radom, sensing a trap and worried that the prisoners they took for this work detail would be killed enroute. But my mom was determined to reunite with what remained of her family and felt she had to take the chance to get back to Radom. He then told her, "Alright, go, but if we both live I will find you, wherever you are."

My mom, by the way, remained working in Radom until she was taken to Auschwitz in the summer of 1944. Sadly, her older sister Regina, along with her husband and their precocious 4-year-old (the only first cousin I would ever have) were murdered there – my mother and Aunt Frances sent to the right and my Aunt Regina and little Hadassah to the left.

In the selection process, the left line meant immediate death in the gas chambers and the right meant life, though for most even that would end within weeks or months in death from starvation, hard labor or the gas chamber. Parents would often be sent in one direction, children in the other, typically to a frightening and lonely death.

Of her family, only my mom and Frances would survive the Nazis. Of my father's family, it was just him and a few cousins.

After Blizyn, my father was sent to the Płaszow-Krakow concentration camp in the spring of 1944. It was here that the following occurred:

Radom native and survivor Joseph Horn, a friend of our family, wrote about my dad in his memoir *Mark It With a Stone: A Moving Account of a Young Boy's Struggle to Survive the Nazi Death Camps* (Barricade Books, 1996). On pages 102-3, he wrote:

"We all knew David well. He was older, in his thirties, had a Chassidic background and was well-versed in Torah. He always carried himself with a certain integrity that comes with knowledge and education, even when he was simply begging for food, as he was tonight."

When they shared their sparse rations with him, he took a few bites, then rose, saying, "You must excuse me. Good fortune like this I must share with my friend Jan." It turned out that Jan was a famous Russian radio announcer from Bialystok. Later that evening my father returned to Horn's bunk, saying, "I thought I might repay your kindness, if you will permit me."

"David began to sing the most beautiful, wistful Chassidic songs," Horn wrote in his book. "It had been so long since I had heard music that I had forgotten the power it could have. Very quickly, I found myself weeping uncontrollably."

And when he was done singing, my father introduced his friend Jan who also had something to share with the prisoners. He spoke of the recent defeat of the Nazis at Stalingrad and urged their fellow inmates not to give up hope.

This historical detail places the timing of this exchange in February of 1943, when the Nazis were finally defeated after a five-month siege.

1944

By the time summer arrived, the Nazis were steadily losing ground militarily but were only stepping up their killing machine. In August they liquidated what was left of the Lodz ghetto and deported more than 50,000 Jews to death camps including Chelmno and Auschwitz-Birkenau.

This was also the year that Germany occupied Hungary and deported Hungarian Jews as well as the Polish ones who had sought safety there. Most of them were murdered in Auschwitz during the spring and summer of 1944.

During the summer of 1944, my father was transferred to Mauthausen in Austria, which had been built in 1938 in essence to work its prisoners to death (more than half of the 195,00 Jews and others who passed through its gates would never emerge). There my dad would face the final brutal winter of the war, and there freedom would find him in the most surprising way.

CHAPTER 6

Liberation and Beyond

---

*"He divided the sea and caused them to pass through,
and He made the waters stand up like a heap. Then He
led them with the cloud by day and all the night with
a light of fire. He split the rocks in the wilderness and
gave them abundant drink like the ocean depths."*

-- PSALM 78

AS ALLIED TROOPS MOVED ACROSS Europe in the early months of 1945, they were surprised and horrified at what they found. Although the Nazis, knowing they were losing the war, did whatever they could – and in a hurry -- to clear traces of their millions of murders, the skeletal prisoners who had somehow survived the horror did as much as the piles of bodies to open Allied eyes to the enormity of the crime.

In addition to those they found in the camps, the soldiers also encountered on the roads a number of emaciated Jews who had managed to live through the forced marches from the camps in Poland that the Nazis had organized quickly in a desperate attempt to obscure the signs of their "final solution."

Over the years I've been active in the Holocaust memorial movement, especially the March of the Living and the Forum for Dialogue Among Nations, I've had the privilege of meeting – and thanking personally -- many of these heroes: British, Russian, righteous Poles and American soldiers who gave kindness and support to those like my parents who had for so long been treated with an inhuman cruelty.

The first discovery of a major camp by Allied forces actually occurred during the summer of 1944 when the Soviets came upon Majdanek outside of Lublin. Despite all the German attempts to hide the evidence – including a hasty burning of the crematoria – the gas chambers stood as silent accusers. Later that summer the Soviets also discovered the killing machines of Belzec, Sobibor and Treblinka, which had been largely deserted after 1943. By this time the majority of German and Polish Jews were dead.

By January the Soviets had advanced enough to liberate Auschwitz, the largest of the Nazi death camps. Because most of the surviving prisoners – roughly 56,000 – were no longer in the camp, having been pushed out on a "death march," so named due to their brutal conditions (the prisoners were typically denied food, drink and sleep), the soldiers found only a few thousand walking skeletons in the camp. Since an estimated 1.1 million Jews, and thousands of Poles and Romani (Gypsies) had been murdered there, German efforts to hide this fact were less than successful, including the victims' charred remains and their warehoused clothing, shoes and other personal effects.

On a personal note, my mother and aunt were two of the approximately 65,000 Jews of the 450,000 tattooed in Auschwitz who lived to tell the tale. It's a number that fails to take into consideration the vast majority who, like my aunt Regina and little cousin Hadassah, were killed immediately upon entering Auschwitz, not surviving long enough to even be tattooed.

It wasn't until April of 1945 that the British forces were able to liberate camps in northern Germany, including Bergen-Belsen where they found some 60,000 prisoners, a starving population riddled with typhus. Sadly, they were in such a deplorable condition that more than a sixth of them died within a few weeks of being liberated.

And in April the American troops would arrive to rescue the 21,000 surviving prisoners of Buchenwald in Germany before moving onto other German camps, including Dachau and Mauthausen.

The Mauthausen-Gusen camp was one of the first massive concentration camp complexes to be built in Nazi Germany – in 1938 -- and it was also the last to be liberated by the Allies, in early May. It's believed that as many as 320,000 Jews and other Nazi "enemies" were killed there over the years.

This is where my dad saw his first GIs, members of America's Third Army, who liberated the Mauthausen sub-camp of Gunskirchen on May 5, 1945. He was 34 at the time, one of nearly 65,000 prisoners the GIs found in various stages of starvation and disease. Among them were Jews from all over but primarily like my dad from Poland as well as Hungary and the Soviet Union. The high numbers were mostly recently arrived prisoners whom the retreating Nazis had brought in that winter from front-line camps such as Auschwitz. The increased numbers only worsened the situation as scarce end-of-war rations had to stretch further and tight housing and poor sewage systems were breeding grounds for typhus and other deadly diseases.

At Mauthausen, unlike some of the other camps, the gas chambers which had been working full-time for years were still killing prisoners just days before liberation. Others, my dad told us, were taken into rooms designated for murder by hanging or gunshot.

When the GIs arrived, they shipped my dad directly off to Wells Women's Hospital in Austria. There he recuperated and gained some of his weight back. By summer he was ready to be transported with the Jewish (Palestinian) Brigade to Italy. Which is where he was living when he discovered that my mother was still alive, having seen her name on a list of survivors.

After their older sister Regina and little niece Hadassah had been killed in Auschwitz, my mother and her surviving sister Frances had been evacuated by the Germans for slave labor at a munitions factory in Lipstadt. But at the end of March, 1945, when the Germans got word that the Allies were heading in their direction, they rounded up the 400 Jewish women remaining at the camp and forced them on a death march. Word traveled fast among them that the Nazis were planning on taking them to Buchenwald to be killed. Deprived of food, water and rest and being marched in brutally cold temperatures, many of them fell by the wayside.

But the GIs were moving faster than the Germans and the march ended abruptly outside of Kaunitz, Germany where the women were told to lie face-down in the snow and mud. There they stayed until the American Army rescued them. Meanwhile the guards who had been whipping them to move faster ran into the woods and changed into civilian clothes to avoid being arrested by the Allies. The date: April 1, 1945, a day that was both Passover and Easter.

A SURPRISE VISITOR

While my mother and aunt were regaining their weight and strength in Kaunitz, as already mentioned, after my dad recuperated sufficiently in Austria, he was turned over to the Jewish (Palestinian) Brigade, Jews who had fought alongside the British in the British army. He was transported by them, along with his buddy and fellow Mauthausen survivor Herbert Hoffman, to Milan, Italy.

My Dad managed to convince his pal Herb to leave the comforts of post-war Italy and rough it all the way to Germany and the woman he loved – my mother

There Dad requested permission to migrate to Palestine – and thanks to my mother 's compulsion to save every document, I still have his application for citizenship (in Hebrew) dated September 27, 1948. At the time he filled it out, the State of Israel was 4 months old.

While they waited the months it would take to get themselves smuggled into Palestine, my ever-resourceful Dad and Herb opened a small wholesale business buying, selling and trading merchandise. How did they raise the capital? By hiring out as performers, singing and telling jokes to the Allied troops stationed in occupied Italy.

When my dad applied for Israeli citizenship in 1948, the Jewish State was 4 months old. But destiny had other plans for him

Like the rest of the survivors, my Dad was in the habit of poring over the lists of survivors published by ORT and the Red Cross. Everyone was on the lookout for the names and whereabouts of any surviving family, friends and neighbors from their hometowns and anyone they had befriended in the camps or in hiding but lost touch with -- and had no idea of their fates.

The moment my father found my mother's name and town on one of those lists was a fateful one for them and for us. Suddenly his goal of emigrating to Palestine shifted to a focus on tracking down a special survivor named Marilla Freidenreich who was listed as living in Kaunitz, Germany.

By the time my father located her name, my mother had settled into a quiet life in a house she shared with her sister Frances and several other women they had been with on the death march. Remembering his vow to her back in the Blizyn work camp, my dad talked his buddy Herb into coming with him to Germany to help locate this pretty and much younger (by 12 years) woman. In fact my mother still insists her husband had the best powers of persuasion of anyone she'd ever met. He even convinced Herb to cross the Alps with him in pursuit of a woman he had no reason to think would ever love him (since they'd only met twice).

Though I'm uncertain of their exact route, the two men most likely traveled from Milan across the Alps, making their way to Zurich. From there they probably hitchhiked into Germany until they arrived in Kaunitz. And, though completely broke by then, my dad sweet-talked a German taxi driver into driving them to my mom's house by saying his "wife" had the money to pay the fare. (I *said* he was persuasive).

More than seven decades have passed but my mom still recalls her shock when a man she barely knew burst in and planted a kiss on her … and then whispered in her ear: "Give me the money to pay the driver. I'll explain later." Having no cash, she paid him in ration cards. As she likes to say, "Only my husband could do this and have it work."

My father courted my mother for several months. He called her Marilla mostly since that is how he met her as a teen in the Radom ghetto, but in close moments he used her Hebrew name, Malka. And years later, when settled in the United States, he would introduce her to business associates as Marlene.

My parents actually had two weddings, both in Stuttgart, Germany, where they moved in the hope of securing better medical care there for Aunt Frances (the city then being under American control). Hers was a slow recuperation in a convalescent home – vertebrae in her neck had been severely damaged from the beatings she'd sustained in Auschwitz.

The looks on my parents' faces as the rabbi in Stuttgart, Germany reads the *ketubah* (marriage contract) speak volumes about a survivor's legacy of loss set against deep gratitude and a passionate commitment to life

My parents' first wedding was a simple civil ceremony in July of 1946 in Mom's living room. With her sister still hospitalized, my mom opted to wait for a more formal ceremony. For the second, on August 16, 1948, they had a religious wedding presided over by a rabbi, and they were surrounded by other young survivors. In the picture, the woman standing to my mother's right is Sasha Katz, my father's cousin whose son Jay would be my college roommate someday.

My newlywed parents relax on a Stuttgart park bench

That year my parents decided they needed to leave Europe but Israel at the time didn't have the sophisticated medical services my aunt needed.

America seemed like the other good option. But they knew that, to accomplish this, they needed an American sponsor who's a family member. So my father began writing to his old boyhood friend from Kalisz, Manny Duell, who was then living in New York, asking him to sign sponsorship forms as a cousin. By then Manny was a success both in real estate and the ladies' garment business, and he was married to an heiress, Irene Kestenberg Duell, a granddaughter of the Poznanskis, a family of wealthy Jewish Polish manufacturers and retailers.

Fortunately Manny agreed to sponsor my folks and Aunt Frances and so began the arduous and lengthy process of applying for and receiving approval to immigrate to America.

THE JEWS OF POST-HOLOCAUST KALISZ

But while the newlyweds were beginning life together and looking toward a future across the ocean, in terms of Jewish history, my father's hometown of Kalisz was undergoing its own seismic shifts.

Shortly after the war ended, some 344 Jews returned to Kalisz seeking to find lost friends and family and take up where their lives had left off. But, according to survivor testimonies, the Kalisz they returned to in 1945 and 1946 – many having been in DP (displaced persons) camps -- was less than welcoming to its prodigal children.

In 1946 the Relief dispatched native son Joseph Arnold from his new home in the United States back to Kalisz. There, as he recalls in an essay reprinted in the *Kalisz Memorial Book*, Arnold encountered a city that was virtually unchanged from the one he left. The one exception: "Jewish Kalisz had been almost entirely destroyed." And when he saw that the gravestones from the Jewish cemetery had been repurposed to pave the streets, he wrote that, whereas "the Poles all around were walking freely, I hesitated to put my foot down for fear that I might be obliterating the name of a Jew who had lived here; he himself, his father and grandfather."

Arnold was horrified at what he found in the old Jewish neighborhood including the pile of rubble that was once the Great Synagogue. Of the hospital and House of Study there was not even a trace, he reported, and Poles were working and living in buildings that once belonged to Jews. "They had murdered and had also inherited," he wrote. Of the 290 ragged survivors he found there, most longed to leave. And for those who insisted on staying, the Relief was able to give some funds to get them back on their financial feet. The once-powerful Jewish philanthropy – now operated from afar -- also sent help to the Kaliszers stuck in Displaced Person Camps in Italy, Austria and Germany.

It was the pogrom there during the summer of 1946 that was the final straw for many of these last Jews of Kalisz. A group identifying themselves as policemen pounded on the door of a building housing many of the survivors. Once inside, they forced Jews up against a wall and began pushing them amid shouted insults. In the end, several Jews were beaten, one critically, before Russian soldiers eventually responded to a plea for help. The incident was enough to convince the lingering survivors that it was time to leave, most of them making their way to Palestine/Israel, the United States or Canada although some moved to larger – and hopefully more welcoming – Polish cities.

STAYING CONNECTED

Although they were scattered through North America and Israel, after everything they'd lived through, the surviving Jews from Kalisz were determined not to lose touch with each other. But, in the days before emails and when international calling was beyond most budgets, that meant lengthy letters and the occasional visit.

In fact, Kalisz ex-pats were already linked well before the war broke out. Beginning in the 1920s, following a wave of immigration that gained momentum after 1900, the organizations of Kalisz-born Jews were potent forces in Palestine/Israel, the US, Canada and as far away as Australia – the earliest on record being a New York-based one which began in 1887. These groups were not purely social but also sent money and sometimes warm clothing back to family, friends and neighbors in their hometown. Another important function was helping immigrants from Kalisz establish lives in their new homes, be that in the US, Canada or Israel. This included sponsoring them as "family" as Manny Duell did for my parents and aunt, as well as finding them housing, English classes and jobs.

This function – especially the sponsoring -- was a lifesaver beginning in the 1930s when Kalisz Jews were increasingly desperate to leave Poland.

And after the war ended, and it became painfully clear the fate of those who had remained in Kalisz, there was an ongoing effort by their brethren who had left before the Nazi net fell over the Jews to get the survivors out of Poland and into Israel, the United States or Canada. Ex-pats around the world rallied to sponsor, welcome and help settle the survivors. In addition, in a poignant role reversal, whereas in the past the Jews of Kalisz had sent help to their former neighbors struggling to build lives for themselves in Israel, after the war, the now-established Israelis were sending help to the survivors still in Poland and elsewhere in Europe.

And not only did the Kalisz-born Israelis help the refugees settle in Israel and send money to those still stuck in Europe, but they often shipped over ritual objects to replace those that had been stolen from the Jews during the Holocaust, including mezuzahs for doorposts and Torahs and tefillin for traditional prayer.

Others in these ex-pat organizations focused on keeping the history and memory of this once-strong Jewish community alive for future generations. In the early '50s those living elsewhere donated large sums to planting a Forest in Memory of the Kalisz Martyrs in the Jerusalem Forest with even those as far away as Australia donating memorial stones.

Over the years, relief funds continued to funnel support to those in need and get-togethers of Kalisz natives were also held across the US, Canada and Israel, especially during the holidays. I can tell you from watching them when I was a kid that survivors know how to celebrate at *simchas* – weddings and bar and bat mitzvahs. In fact, I've never seen anyone have a better time.

These ex-pat communities also donated Torahs to the fledgling Israeli state's synagogues, in memory of the slain. Other projects included a Kalisz House in Tel Aviv to serve as a reminder of the community that had been destroyed.

Anyone interested in understanding this fallen community will appreciate a thick book of reminiscences, histories and photos known as the *Kalisz Memorial Book: The History of the Jews in Kalish*. This remarkable volume was collected, compiled and edited by I.M. Lask, a colleague of my father's back in the day when he was doing business in Kalisz. Including the reports of Kaliszers Dr. Moshe Gross (Henryk Zeligowski), Wolf Lassman,

S. Glickman, Abraham Milgrim, Dov Zielonka and Halina Liebeskind as well as the Ringelblum Archives, the book is a terrific resource and makes the life of Kalisz's Jews during these difficult years come alive, both the joys and the sorrows. I recently ordered a copy as an on-demand reprint through the Yiddish Book Center's David and Sylvia Steiner Yizkor Book Collection at http://www.yiddishbookcenter.org/collections/yizkor-books.

Although nowhere near as complete or in-depth, other books have attempted to convey the story of Jewish Kalisz. The aforementioned *Recollections of Edith Gomolka* (Richard Gomolka, 2016) is a poignant and beautifully written first-person account of a young girl's escape from Kalisz with her mother into the rigors of life in Russia. Especially powerful are the scenes towards the end of the memoir depicting what they found when returning to Kalisz at war's end: the complete erasure of what was just six years earlier a bustling and vibrant Jewish community.

One example of Kalisz-based historical fiction is Rosalind Brenner's novel *Kalisz: A Journey of Return* (Trafford Publishing, 2013), which was inspired by her father's life. Featured is a family whose son follows the Zionist dream, which was embraced by especially the young during the first half of the 20th century. Despite the hardships of life in Palestine/Israel during the 1940s, the move from Kalisz to Israel ultimately saved the young protagonist's life, as it did for so many of the other seemingly radical youth of that time and place who left home to weather the hardships of the Promised Land.

But by 1949, a world away from his hometown of Kalisz, my father was beginning to carve out a very different kind of life for himself, my mother and, soon enough, for my sister and myself.

———

CHAPTER 7

New Life: The Years that Followed

---

*"Elijah picked up the child and brought him down from
the upper room into the main room, and gave him to
his mother. 'See,' said Elijah. 'Your son is alive.'"*

– KINGS 1-17

COMING TO AMERICA

BY 1949 MANNY DUELL AND his wife Irene had been in the United
States for more than a decade and were living every immigrant's
dream in a fashionable apartment on Manhattan's Fifth Avenue.
And, because they had escaped before Hitler's net engulfed
Europe, they were somewhat detached from the scope, horror
and impact it had on their Jewish landsmen.

You can imagine the stark contrast between their frame of
reference in 1949 and that of my parents and aunt.

Manny's initial response to my dad's request for sponsorship was to send him a gift pack of Gillette razors and a fairly
discouraging letter stating that many a Pole was dismayed that
the streets of America were not paved with gold, but with the

hard work and tough living conditions that they faced once they arrived here.

**The well-to-do Duells sponsored my parents and aunt for
immigration, making their American dream a reality**

He pointed out the Jewish immigrants who had come before, many of whom had held important or prosperous positions before the war in Poland, soon learned that opportunity knocked only for those who were willing to start at the bottom and struggle, often putting in long hours under inhumane working conditions. And sometimes not even for them.

But my parents were not to be easily discouraged. They wrote back that they well understood the challenges facing them in this new land, and stated both of their willingness to work hard and do whatever it took to succeed here. They could not fully commit for my Aunt Frances, however, who was still recovering from typhoid fever and the beatings she had gotten at the hands of the Nazis in the camps (Fortunately, after immigrating, she was destined to regain her strength, marry a wonderful man and become a successful retailer in her own right).

In addition, my parents pledged that they would gladly repay Manny Duell (formerly Dunkelman) for any out-of-pocket expenses involved in sponsoring the three of them. They had every confidence they would be able to do this since one of the functions that Manny was required to perform as their sponsoring "relative" was to guarantee employment. This was designed to ensure the new immigrants would be contributing members of the American economy, and not dependent on others or the government for their daily bread.

My parents and aunt all rejoiced when Manny signed the sponsorship forms and they shared their good news with their fellow survivors in Stuttgart. But even after Manny signed on, it took months of filing forms and wrestling with the bureaucracy of immigration before my dad and mom and Frances were finally approved to enter the United States.

At long last the bureaucratic quagmire was over and my parents and Aunt Francis left Remenhofen, Germany during the last week of February, 1949 aboard a military transport boat named "The General Muir." By all reports it was a rough crossing, with both my aunt and father felled with violent bouts of sea sickness and my mother running between the two of them. By the time the boat docked in New York Harbor on March 11, 1949, Aunt Frances was so weak from the rough seas that she had to be off-loaded in a wheel chair. That day Manny failed to materialize but a woman, who turned out to be his wife Irene arrived at the pier asking for a Mr. Kempner and explaining (in the French which only she and my mother understood -- my mother also speaks Polish, Yiddish, German and her adopted English) that Mr. Duell was in Paris on business and that she would help them get settled. Later they spoke Polish which all four of them understood.

So began an association that would span the years, an often classic formula of good intentions mixed with misunderstanding that can typify relations between the haves and the have-nots.

Irene hailed a cab at the pier, instructing the driver (now speaking an English the newcomers did not understand) to drop them and their belongings at the Chesterfield Hotel near 49th street in the Rockefeller Center area of Manhattan. At the hotel they secured one room for two weeks on the 19th floor for $35 per week until they could find a permanent address, a sum that quickly depleted their meager savings.

One detail they never forgot: Irene took them out to dinner that night to a fancy New York restaurant and ordered them all grapefruit which they had never seen much less tasted before. Instead of being impressed, they found it to be sour, but masked their distaste and expressed their gratitude nonetheless.

MAKING DO: HARD LABOR, LOW WAGES IN AMERICA

True to his word, Manny gave my dad a job in his garment factory. My father started out as a shipping clerk and eventually moved up the ladder to the more prestigious position of fabric cutter making $35 per week. My mother also found employment as a hat designer, a skill that had served her well (and repeatedly saved her life) during her years in the camps.

Dad was delighted to be a father and we spent many happy times together as in this early photo in Washington Heights

Their somewhat scant salaries necessitated a move into a small apartment in North Bergen, N.J. which cost the family $12 per week. The $35 per week salary had to support all three adults and my father's cost to travel to work in New York by train along with his extravagant habits of smoking cigarettes, wearing dapper suits and keeping his shoes shined.

When their landlady in North Bergen demanded a raise in rental of $5.00 per week to pay for housing a third person, Aunt Frances, the decision was made to move to New York. In June of 1949 they first occupied their Upper West Side apartment, a sixth-floor walk-up at 659 W. 162nd Street in Washington Heights.

Not content to stay put as a cutter, around the same time I came along in 1950 my father worked hard to prove valuable to Manny in the areas of product design, production and sales. He was also able to maximize those all-important customer and supplier relationships much to Manny's advantage.

THE FAMILY FACES NEAR TRAGEDY AND OVERCOMES AGAIN

We took a family vacation in 1953 to Toronto. There we visited two of my mom's surviving friends from her hometown of

Radom. And she'd grown even closer to sisters Ella and Guta Lederman while they were all together in Stuttgart after the war.

But during what should have been a happy trip for the family, my father took very sick and we had to return quickly to the United States. The neurologist diagnosed him with a benign brain tumor that seriously affected his sight and sense of balance.

On May 27, my dad underwent a risky neurosurgery at New York's Columbia Presbyterian Hospital. This operation proved to be a huge setback for our family. Not only did I nearly lose my dad when I was only 2 years old, but following the brain surgery, my mother was told by the neurologist that my father would never be able to return to any kind of strenuous manual labor. Knowing she'd need to work full-time to support our family, my mother contacted her old boss and returned to her career in the millinery field designing hats, a position she had put on hold after I was born.

My father underwent a long recuperation period following his brain surgery. During that summer our family joined my dad who was slowly regaining his strength at the vacation home of my dad's cousins the Wolkovich sisters, Sadie and Mary, in Elba Ron N.J. These cousins – by then Sadie had married Israel Diament and Mary had married Max Smullen -- had also done much to welcome my parents into their homes and their lives in their early years in the US.

OUR FAMILY CLOUD'S SILVER LINING: THE BIRTH OF KERO

After his lengthy recuperation, my dad's working relationship with Manny Duell had ended. And, when the family returned to

New York in August of 1953 following my third birthday, my parents were approached by another survivor, Isaac Rosen, whose mother had been a friend of my mom's in the camps and with whom she'd stayed close over the years.

Isaac was 13 years my dad's junior and looked up to him as a mentor. He proposed combining his own youthful energy with my dad's business contacts, savvy and knowledge of the women's garment industry. My mother trusted Isaac and encouraged my father to join forces with him. So they structured a business where my father would play the executive role and Isaac the operations manager one. And KERO Lingerie (KEmpner-ROsen) was born. Their factory was opened on 26th street at Madison Avenue in September, 1953 a month before my father's 43rd birthday. Based upon my Dad's solid reputation, he was able to secure a $100,000 line of credit from the Chase Manhattan bank to buy equipment and fabric.

KERO soon became very successful as my dad worked harder than he should have and kept costs down by designing, selling and even delivering merchandise himself whenever the need arose. He also made a habit of paying his bills early to take discounts off invoices and further reduce their costs. Within a short time he had built the confidence of his suppliers that he would pay on time, gaining KERO increasingly favorable terms and opportunities to buy at below-market prices. The resulting competitive pricing KERO offered retailers won them deals with such emerging discounters as the Ben Franklin stores (where Wal-Mart's Sam Walton got his start as a store manager). The upshot: Within five years, KERO had over 60 employees and my folks – along with the Rosens -- were making enough to put aside some savings for their future.

THE KEMPNERS RAISE AN AMERICAN FAMILY

Nearly a decade after I was born on July 30th, 1950, my sister Tes entered the world on May 27th, 1960. We were both named after murdered grandparents, my parents' sincerest hope being that, through our lives, their own parents' legacies would live on. And we were still at 659 W. 162 Street, an apartment we would remain in for 16 years. When I was old enough for school they sent me to Yeshiva Rabbi Moses Solovechik near Yeshiva University in Manhattan for first and second grade and by third grade I was enrolled in Public School 128. But by the time I had completed elementary school our Upper West Side neighborhood was losing its Jewish character and transforming into the Spanish Harlem it remains to this day.

Luckily my grades were good enough to qualify me along with several of my Jewish pals to attend the prestigious Junior High School 80 in the Bronx which specialized in math and science.

Now the time had come for my survivor parents to truly enjoy living the American dream. For them this included winter getaways to Florida and Passovers and summers in the Catskills at various kosher hotels and bungalow colonies.

MY DAD'S SURVIVING RELATIVES

They also worked hard at keeping in touch with remaining relatives and friends from both their hometowns and the camps. On my dad's side of the family, there were the Diaments and

Smullens, the cousins who provided so much support and love during those first insecure years in America and then again during and after my dad's emergency brain surgery. After losing so many of their relatives, survivors tended to embrace even distant family and cousins by marriage, especially when they were landsmen, coming from the same town. For my folks, this included the Arkushes, who were related to Max Smullen and also hailed from Kalisz.

In addition, my dad had Zalc and Wolkovich cousins living in Paris and Rouene, France whom they remained in touch with and with whom they even managed the occasional visit over the years.

And then there was the Israeli branch of my dad's family.

In 1956, my parents attended a Jewish National Fund (JNF) presentation at a meeting of the Kalisher Society, an organization that brought survivors together to memorialize the dead and help the living. On that night the featured speaker for the JNS was an Israeli named Channah Vardimon. During her talk, her young son turned to his dad and, pointing to my father, said in a loud voice, "That man looks like my zayde (grandfather)!"

Amazing for my father to discover his Israeli cousin Channah Wolkovich Vardimon leading a Jewish National Fund meeting in 1956

And for good reason. My father, they discovered that night, was no less than the nephew of the little boy's zayde.

Remember the story of how my paternal grandfather Meyer

Kempner joined his brother-in-law, Abraham Wolkovich in Israel for several months circa 1928, planning to send for my grandmother and my then-teenaged dad when he got settled? Remember the "warning" my grandfather received at the hands of the Arabs who cut off his big toe and told him, "Jew, go back to Poland"? Remember how he took the message seriously, returning to the "safety of Poland," a move that would cost him his life – and that of my grandmother – at the hands of the Nazis some 15 years later?

It turned out that the speaker's full name was Channah Wolkovich Vardimon and she was Abraham's daughter. Her young son – who was about my age -- was struck by the strong family resemblance between my dad and his grandfather back in Israel, my dad's uncle Abraham Wolkovich, whose move there most likely saved his life.

I continue to be struck by the irony: Most of the Zionist risk-takers who turned their backs on the "safety" of Eastern Europe to battle disease, poverty and the Arabs in the wilds of then-Palestine lived and today, like the Vardimons, have children and grandchildren (most of whom speak Hebrew) to continue to grow their family trees.

THE BEST OF TIMES AND THE WORST OF TIMES

All was going well until 1962, the year before my bar mitzvah. My dad had developed a rapidly growing tumor on his back which was eventually diagnosed as malignant and had to be quickly removed. Following two surgeries and another lengthy convalescent period that kept him away from the business, Dad did recuperate. But he was forced to dissolve his business partnership with Isaac Rosen. KERO Lingerie was no more.

Fortunately, during the decade of KERO, we had not only lived well but my dad had managed to invest in real estate in Toronto, a house in Rego Park, an apartment in South Miami Beach and property in Cape Coral, Florida. He also began to invest heavily in the stock market.

Although my dad had no visible or traditional means of support beyond social security, some German reparations payments and his own investment income, he would often tell us that he was grateful to be a survivor of both the Holocaust and two serious operations. He was happy to be alive, he loved my mom and was proud to have both a 3-year-old daughter he adored and a son of bar mitzvah age to carry on the family name.

Having suffered two near fatal illnesses, my dad along with my mom opted to throw me a first-rate bar mitzvah the size and cost of which mirrored that of a sizable wedding. My bar mitzvah reception took place on August 4, 1963 at the Park Terrace Caterers opposite Yankee stadium in the Bronx. It was a lavish affair for 300 friends and relatives replete with a seven-course dinner and a full band, with staged movies and photos to capture this historic Kempner event.

In addition, a move was in our future. My parents had invested in a new home in Rego Park beginning in 1959 but did not occupy it until 1965. Instead they had rented it out for additional income to help pay off the mortgage.

Though they had not been ready to leave the convenience of apartment living in Manhattan as long as my dad co-owned KERO and worked on Madison Avenue, after the company was dissolved, my parents were free to move. They also realized around this time that the Jewish population was shifting to the suburbs – including Long Island, Queens and Yonkers – in search of bigger homes and better schools, and we followed suit.

The timing was right for my folks. My sister was ready to enter kindergarten and I needed the kind of high school that could prepare me for college, a training ground for living the American dream that my survivor parents were very keen on. So they gave their tenants notice to leave and arranged to move into their row house at 64-06 Wetherole Street in Rego Park during the spring of 1965. Tes attended the elementary school directly across the street from our new home and I enrolled in Forest Hill High School.

But my father was not one to slink into retirement at age 55. In 1965, with my mom's encouragement, he would ride the subway to Wall Street every day, studying to become a stockbroker. While he initially failed the collegiate level stock broker license exam, Dad being Dad, he resolved to do better and study harder. And true to form, applying the full force of his smarts and determination, he passed on his second try.

So at age 55, this son of Kalisz with a high school education who had lost his family and friends in the Shoah and come nearly penniless to the US a mere 16 years earlier without a word of English, was embarking on a new career. Here, in the land of opportunity, my dad was now a stockbroker for Edward A. Viner & Company. Truly an inspiration to all of us who would follow him.

DAVID KEMPNER: THE LEGACY

Despite his many health setbacks my father lived long enough to see me attend the University of Miami and graduate from New York University's School of Commerce. He was so proud that his son was the first member of his family to graduate from college.

My dad also lived long enough to see me marry Mindy in 1971 and the births of his three grandchildren whom he adored. He also saw my sister Tes graduate from Queens's College and become a bride. In his later years, my father witnessed with great joy all three of his grandchildren becoming bat and bar mitzvah. It was a great satisfaction to him knowing that the Kempner family's *etz chaim* (tree of life) was not cut off at the roots in Poland but instead was transplanted into the strong and fertile soil of opportunity and tolerance here in the United States of America.

My father and mother adored their grandchildren and despite the miles that usually separated them, always managed to be close throughout the years. This is Benjay they have their arms around

A special source of pride for my father was living to see his son achieve the position of Vice President of Sales for the Gillette Company (remember how his first gift from America when they were still in Germany was a package of Gillette razors from Manny Duell?). He was immensely grateful to have the Kempner name rise from the ashes and ruin of the Holocaust to the executive suite of a Fortune 500 company.

On a global scale, my dad lived to witness the birth of the State of Israel, the Jewish homeland he had dreamed of when he was young. He watched as Jewish soldiers successfully defended this promised land in five bloody-but-miraculous wars (in 1948, 1956, 1967, 1973 and 1980).

David Kempner died at the age of 88 on January 25, 1999 in Rego Park, N.Y. while he and my mom were waiting for a taxi to take them to the airport and their winter vacation apartment in Miami Beach.

My mom visits my dad in the New Montefiore Cemetery

Sadly, he died before he could see his first grandchild Batyah married, but he was keenly aware of her love for and intention to marry Benji Cohen, a match he heartily endorsed. No doubt he is looking down from heaven appreciatively at the thriving Jewish families – 11 great-grandchildren to date -- being created by the three grandchildren -- Batyah, Benjay and Jeremy -- he loved so dearly.

After my dad died, my mom wrote:

"David embodied the perfect blend of old world ethics and applied wisdom with modern forward thinking. He was an impeccable dresser, a great storyteller, a terrific showman, a devoted son with many friends and he danced like a dream.

When I saw him in 1943 in Blizyn, I noticed that, even in the camps, David maintained his dignity and was sought after by other inmates for comforting words of Torah and deep under-standing of Talmudic teaching. He nourished his friends' bod-ies by sharing his meager rations and their souls by sharing his melodious voice, softly singing *z'miros* (mystical Jewish melodies) into the night.

He vowed that if we both survived, he would find me. And true to his word he did just that. As his wife and partner for 52 years, my love and respect for him continues to grow with each passing day. *Zicrono livracha*, may his memory be for a blessing."

David Kempner is buried at:

New Montefiore Cemetery

Block #3, Section #4, Row A, Grave 2L

Pine Lawn, Long Island

Since he loved both singing and his people so much, if you visit, please sing Dad a rousing chorus of *Am Yisraol Chai* (*The People of Israel Lives*). You can also join me in offering up a prayer of gratitude for him and all the survivors who stayed strong and true to their Jewish faith despite all the hardships they endured.

For never giving up, for paving the way to a bright future and passing on to all of us their spirit of courage, love and pride.

CHAPTER 8

Kalisz After the War and Today

———

"And the Lord will strike Egypt, striking and healing,
and they will return to the Lord, and He will listen
to their pleas for mercy and heal them."

-- ISAIAH 19:21-25

A PLEASANT AND PICTURESQUE CITY with a selection of river vistas to greet the eye, today's Kalisz boasts a top university, a soft drink plant, factories that produce jeans and plane engines and 18 churches. What's more, the city's women's volleyball team went on to become the Polish national champions in 2005.

In the city's official English-language website, "Kalisz: The Oldest Town in Poland!" there is much to learn about ancient days. As well as this note: "During the history the town has been worried by many pests, floods, fires and turmoil of war. But it always revived, keeping its range and gaining in value. In August 1914 the Prussian army shot at, bombarded and then set fire to Kalisz for unknown reasons. As a result of this tragedy nearly the entire historical city center lay in ruins."

**Kalisz is an up-to-date Polish city with a healthy
economy and a number of pretty views**

But the only reference to World War II is: "During World War II Kalisz was incorporated into an area that was called 'Warthegau' by the Germans. The Nazi occupation was a period of oppression and discrimination for Kalisz people." No mention of the decimation of a third of its population: the Jewish community.

Interestingly, in the Polish edition of the official Kalisz website, there *is* an article. When translated into English, the reader can see that the article reports on the city's absorption into the Reich in the autumn of 1939: "The Polish language was banned, Polish names were erased, monuments removed. The society suffered from repressions, terror, mass executions. The occupation brought many sufferings to the citizens." It also goes on to state: "It was a tragic last chapter in the history of Kalisz Jewry, with persecution and total destruction. In November, 1939 the Nazis created a ghetto between Targowa, Pow, Chopina and Wodna streets. Some Jews were transported to the General

Government, many perished in camps in Beł ec, Majdanek, Sobibór, Chełmno upon Ner, Treblinka and Birkenau. Others were killed in car-gas chambers. In July, 1942 the 150 remaining Jews were transported to the Litzmannstadt ghetto. The world of Kalisz's Jews, existing for 800 years, has been ruthlessly destroyed." And, as a postscript, it reads: "The Jewish district has survived the war, but its inhabitants have never come back to Złota, Ciasna, Chopina or Kanonicka Street. It is the time to bring back their memory and give evidence to our common history."

After the Shoah

Still, the welcome the roughly 2,000 returning survivors received at war's end was lukewarm at best. Among the first of the returnees were those who made it their business to reopen the city's Jewish Committee. By registering with the Committee survivors were entitled to assistance with such resettlement needs as housing, jobs, training, education and other basic necessities.

In addition, between 1946-1947, some 150 other Kalisz natives were repatriated from the Soviet Union, Jews like Edith Gomolka and her mother who had managed to survive the war there and returned to Kalisz in the hopes of finding friends and family. Some of them also attempted to reclaim some of their property.

There were certainly among this rag-tag crew those who, anticipating they could pick up the lives they had left behind, planned on staying. Whereas for others post-war Kalisz was seen as a temporary stop enroute to greener pastures such as the US, Canada, pre-Israel Palestine, South Africa and larger cities in Poland.

In the earliest days of the Committee's post-liberation work, the first wave of returnees were concentration camp survivors from Auschwitz-Birkenau, Teresin, Buchenwald, Mauthausen and Bergen-Belsen, as well as Ravensbrück and Dachau, some 337 Jews in all. The records show another 66 Jews returned from the Polish army, and 19 had been resistance fighters. Later, most returnees were those coming back from the USSR. Between 1945-1950, 1,278 Jewish Kaliszers were registered by the Committee, a number destined to climb eventually to 2,270 survivors in all. No one knows how many others came and left quickly, heading for more welcoming locales before even so much as registering with the committee.

The vast majority of those who did register were adults, but records reveal there were also 116 children born during the war years in the USSR. Among those registered in the city were transients, though most of them (1,277) named Kalisz and surroundings as their home before that fateful autumn of 1939. They tended to be craftsmen including tailors, cobblers, mechanics, electricians and a range of merchants. Interesting that few professionals such as lawyers, doctors and professors returned to reclaim Kalisz as their home, even temporarily.

The first task the Committee took on for returnees was simply feeding and housing them, plus transporting them upon arrival to temporary shelters. They were also intent on recording data on every Jew who reentered the city and making sure they received what was theirs by law. Each former concentration camp prisoner was entitled to up to 20,000 zloty. Jews returning from the USSR took home anywhere from 2,000 and 10,000 zloty, in addition to allotments of food and clothing.

In her memoir, Kalisz native Edith Gomolka noted that, more than a plea for support, the main purpose of registering was the hope of finding surviving loved ones. "People were desperately looking for someone dear, even for any familiar faces," she wrote. "But most of the time, alas, with no results. The ones who left Poland after the war who registered with the center, fled the country in despair. They listed their names for the Committee's records in case someone was seeking them out."

Another task the Committee took on was trying in some small measure to recreate opportunities for Jews to worship. To accomplish this, several leaders were elected in 1945 to run the Kalisz Religious Assembly, including a kosher butcher. In 1946 the Assembly became the Jewish Faith Congregations. Either way, the primary challenge of reconstructing Jewish life was the lack of a synagogue, as they had all been demolished. The best option at the time: a prayer room in a home on Listopada Street. Other Committee responsibilities included overseeing the Jewish cemetery and making sure the elderly and infirm had adequate food, shelter and heat.

In the kind of abrupt and ironic flip of fate that Jewish history is known for, after decades of the Jews of the city sending aid to the Kalisz natives struggling to eke out a living in pre-Israel Palestine, there were now aid packages coming the other way: from former Kaliszers living there, who had formed their own Kalisz Aid Committee.

But, in addition to helping ease resettlement, the city's Jewish Committee had a far more grim task. In November of 1945, the Committee oversaw the exhumation of some 1,500 Kalisz Jews killed in gas chamber trucks. The mass graves were discovered in the forests around Kalisz and the Committee saw to it that the bodies were reinterred in the city's Jewish cemetery.

To give you an idea of what my father or another Kalisz Jew would have seen had he or she walked into town after the war, here is an excerpt from a letter dated November 1945. It was sent by an anonymous Committee member to a group of concerned former Kaliszers living in Palestine:

"After returning to Kalisz the lone person finds no one from his family there, getting the impression that he is now living in a cemetery, when the cemetery would only be visited once a year. These people desire warmth, care, and their own environment. Both synagogues have been destroyed, the old cemetery has been levelled, the stones from it were used to line the banks of the Prosna River, the second cemetery exists only partially. The hospital and mikveh are gone. The cemetery does not have a wall. Every Jew returning to Kalisz receives accommodation and a one-time aid of 300 zlotys. We run a canteen, provide two-course meals. Special care is given to the sick. The Religious Assembly exists alongside the Jewish Committee. The Committee also runs a lodging house."

As in other cities across Poland, help to returnees also came through other sources including ORT. A clinic that would remain operative until 1950 was housed on Listopada Street along with a kindergarten with 13 small students in the spring of 1946. At the time 26 Jewish orphans also lived in the Kalisz children's home. In addition, ORT conducted training for survivors in such professions as tailor, glassmaker and car mechanic.

But most of the Jews who decided to stay in town – at least for the time being – worked in Jewish cooperatives which, two years after the war's end, manufactured such consumer goods as clothing and shoes and other leather goods.

And, despite their tiny numbers, there were survivors who got involved in local politics, once an area of some Jewish influence, as befitting a population that once made up nearly a third of the city. Though many of the old parties regrouped, including Poale Zion and the Bund, they were hardly a force to be reckoned with.

But despite the activities of the Committee, ORT and other well-intentioned individuals, at the end of the day, the vast majority of the 2,000-plus area Jews who miraculously survived the Shoah and opted to return to Kalisz ultimately decided that it was too hard to remain in a city and country where their families had been murdered, their community decimated and their world destroyed. And which had virtually no Jewish infrastructure left to build new lives around.

Leon Solnik wrote at the time: "The Jewish community of Kalisz lived an autonomous national life of its own. All of this has been eradicated. The Jews were murdered, their property pillaged, their homes destroyed ... even the old cemetery has vanished, covered by new buildings."

About her own brief return in 1945, Gomolka wrote, "As far as the eye could see, nothing was added, nothing was demolished, not even the colors had been changed... yet something had changed. There was no life left in the town." As she walked the streets of Kalisz's once-Jewish neighborhood with her cousin, the only other survivor of their family, she saw with horror rows of gravestones that had been uprooted from the Jewish cemetery and laid along the riverbed. "Now, in this ghost town, was the Jews' existence was erased. Neither the living nor the dead was here. Only the tombstones on the Prosna River would remain for those passersby to tell what once was." And, as they walked further, she asked him, "Where is the synagogue? It should be there. Am I hallucinating?"

'No, you aren't hallucinating,' he said. 'The synagogue was burnt and leveled to the ground. Now in its place they added an addition to Town Hall.'"

Compounding this immense sense of loss was the often less-than-welcoming attitude of their neighbors. Anti-Semitism had reared its ugly head once more.

During the summer of 1946, a building on Listopada Street housed a number of survivors. One August day a group of people saying they were the police pounded on the door. Once admitted, they told the Jews to line up and shoved them against the wall. After a woman began shouting from the window, and Russian soldiers were cajoled by a Jew and Army doctor to enter the building, an arrest was finally made but not until several Jews were beaten.

At around the same time news reached the returnees' ears about a pogrom in nearby Kielce. "One would think that after the cruel and sadistic German occupation that the world would change," Gomolka wrote in her memoir. "How could they inflict so much pain in this massacre and mayhem upon the survivors? The news of this pogrom came as a big blow to all the Jews who were left in Poland... now we mourned not only the victims of World War II but now the Jews of Kielce. The viciousness affected us all tremendously..."

Indeed for many these attacks represented the final straw. By 1946, nearly all those Jews remaining in Kalisz were convinced that "you can't go home again." By the end of that year, barely 300 Jews remained in the city. The rest had opted to move on, voting with their feet that it was hopeless trying to resurrect their old lives there. For most, it was just too hard to live in the midst of all that loss. "We found out with sadness and a lake of tears reserved just for this moment that everyone from our family, our friends, the entire town of Jews had perished," Gomolka wrote. "We literally lost hundreds of relatives."

DEMOCRACY COMES TO POLAND

In 1989, exactly a half-century after the German invasion, the Polish government was transformed into a democracy and the country underwent a seismic shift. However, the changes for those few Jews who remained and those who came later – as well as those who timidly stepped forward from the shadows of Polish life – were slow and subtle. But they were nonetheless real.

It took a decade following the fall of the communist People's Republic of Poland and the birth of the democratic government Third Polish Republic for Poland to join NATO (1999) and the European Union.

In 1990 American-born Rabbi Michael Schudrich began working in Poland in outreach and in 2004 he became the Chief Rabbi of Poland, ushering in a new air of opportunity. "After democracy took hold, Poland became more open to Jews, even after 90 percent were killed by the Germans," the rabbi told us. "Pope John Paul II fought anti-Semitism, opening the door for Jewish life here. Many of the survivors had fled into the Soviet Union during the War and then returned after it was over," he says. "And many others came out of the closet, where they'd been hidden Jews." Of these Jews, tens of thousands had either kept their Jewish faith from their children until now or had been adopted out to Polish families to save them during the Holocaust and were now learning their true identity, the rabbi adds. "With things changing, their adoptive parents or neighbors often told them decades later, saying now it was safe for them to know they are Jews."

Rabbi Schudrich regularly hears from those who have only recently become aware of their Jewish roots. "Many of them come to me to learn more and, if their Judaism is only on their father's side, often to convert. One blessing of democracy is that minorities can thrive," he adds. "And Poland is fighting their anti-Semitic past."

Kalisz however, has yet to develop synagogue life, the rabbi reports, with the closest one being in Lodz, an hour and 40 minutes away by car followed by Warsaw, roughly a two-hour drive.

WHICH JEWISH SITES ARE STILL VISIBLE?

Unlike many other cities in Poland, there are no existing structures that clearly show Kalisz's vibrant Jewish past. Indeed, the visitor looking for signs of 800 years of Jewish life in Kalisz will have some sleuthing to do.

In front of the now filled-in tributary

Visitors *can* visit the Park of the Book (which I have done). It was built over the filled-in tributary on the piece of land that once held the Great Synagogue, which dated back to 1859.

My father became a bar mitzvah within the walls of that once-magnificent building in 1923, a full 16 years before the Nazis tore it down. Much of the materials: the lumber and stone from what remains even by today's standards a large and impressive structure, was used, along with Jewish prayer books and ritual objects, and books from Polish libraries as well, to fill in the river bed on the site that is now this park. You will see a marker here describing how the tributary was filled up with books. Standing here in the park you can imagine the Great Synagogue reigning over this spot in its majestic splendor. This location later housed the Communist Party headquarters in the years following the war and now a bank stands here.

With Professor Swladomer and a student at the site of one of the synagogues destroyed by the Nazis

Though the city's historic old Jewish cemetery on Nowy Swiat Street was destroyed by the Nazis and is mostly covered over at this point (more on that later), the newer one, containing tombstones from the 19th and 20th centuries, though in poor condition and with several tombstones victimized by vandals over the years, can be found on Podmiejska Street. Visitors hoping to see this "new" cemetery as well as a model of the Great Synagogue that, along with some other memorabilia, is housed in a memorial hall there, can make an appointment well in advance with Hila Marcinkowska at Hila@jewish.org.pl. From Poland, her phone number is +48600 067 956.

The new Jewish cemetery in Kalisz is one of the few sites there still visible from the city's eight centuries of Jewish life

The diligent searcher will find a few of the buildings that played such pivotal roles in the lives of the Jews of Kalisz still standing but they have all been repurposed. Observers point to the former Beit Hamidrash (study hall) on the corner of Zlota and Targowa streets which is currently a store selling alcohol and groceries. It's also believed that the Jewish pharmacy which stood at the corner of Babina and Zlota streets has been replaced by a shop selling wedding dresses as well as a new pharmacy. And the former home for the aged at the corner of Piskorzewska and Parczewskiego is now reportedly an abandoned building.

Ciasna Street, which was once a bustling hub of Jewish life with the Polai Zion offices, the Jewish Theater, the Hashomar Hatzair offices, a small synagogue and a mechanics workshop is now largely filled with tenement houses in a neighborhood that is, by all reports, somewhat seedy and unsafe.

Also of interest is the former Young Zionists Training Center at 15 Piskorzewie, with a barn that several observers believe was the former Zionist building. Though the Reform Synagogue of Krotka Street did not survive the war, observers say there is a plan afoot to create a square commemorating the city's destruction in that synagogue's old locale.

Another tip: If exploring the city on foot, it is easier to retrace steps of the Jews of Kalisz if you look out for these street names:

* Zlota Street (formerly Jewish, Pow or Nowa Street)
* Ciasna Street
* Parczewskiego Street, opposite Babina Street (formerly Nadwadna)
* Babina Street
* Piskorzewska Street
* Chopina Street, crossing Wodna Street
* Wodna Street
* Narutowicza Street

* Garbarska Street
* Targowa Street
* New Market Square, West Side (formerly Dekert Square).

If planning a visit to Poland, I recommend getting in touch in advance with the Forum for Dialogue (forum@dialog.org.pl). This Polish nonprofit exists with the goal of fostering communication between Poles and Jews with an eye to "eradicating anti-Semitism and teaching tolerance through education."

With School of Dialogue participants

They accomplish this by educational programs, seminars, publications and exchange programs between Polish and Jewish leaders. In addition, thanks to their growing network of activists across Poland, they are often able to put visitors in contact with those who are involved in preserving Jewish heritage in small towns and former *shtetls*.

Since so little remains of the institutions and buildings, the tours and dialogues grow even more important for both the Poles who live there to understand the city's Jewish influences – and history -- as well as for those who visit in an effort to envision how their parents, grandparents and great-grandparents lived Jewish lives here.

This is why I believe the Forum's School of Dialogue program launched in 2008 to be an important step for raising mutual awareness. Under the supervision of Forum Educators, in 2011, local high school students developed a walking tour of Jewish Kalisz (you may read all about it on Forum's website at www.dialog.org.pl in the School of Dialogue archive).

**Participants in this Forum for Dialogue teen program
learned an immense amount about the lives, history
and fate of the Jews who once lived in Kalisz**

Another important stop is Polin: Museum of the History of Polish Jews (polin@polin.pl), which is located 6 Mordechaja Anielewicza Street in Warsaw. A few hours there will give the visitor an excellent background, preparing them for what they will see -- and more to the point what they won't see -- once arriving in Kalisz.

CONTROVERSY OVER JEWISH REMAINS

The Forum for Dialogue is one expression of many Poles' commitment to recognizing their communities' Jewish pasts. But it's not always an easy process.

In Kalisz, a school and its playground and soccer field were built in the 1960s under Communist rule. These sit atop the old Jewish cemetery on Nowy Swiat Street, its graves dating back many centuries and ending during the late 18th century when overcrowding necessitated the establishment of the "new" Jewish cemetery on Podmiejska Street.

The old cemetery is the repository of much history. In fact one of its graves is said to belong to the prominent 17th-century author and Biblical commentator Rabbi Abraham Abele Gombiner, among the many communal leaders and Torah greats interred here.

In an ongoing push to restore the graves, as the school once used for children with disabilities now stands vacant, Poland's Chief Rabbi Michael Schudrich and other Jewish leaders argue that the playground needs to be relocated to make this restoration possible.

To date, Rabbi Schudrich reports, negotiations, in particular with the mayor's office, have failed to yield any willingness to restore the historic cemetery.

Ironically, the now-deserted school was named for Janusz Korczak who headed up the Jewish orphanage during World War II and insisted on staying with the children all the way to Treblinka where he was murdered along with his young charges.

Elsewhere throughout Poland, Jewish cemetery restoration has been ongoing since democracy came to the country in 1989. And more than 1,400 Jewish graveyards have been found and repaired in the intervening years. In some towns, cooperation and respect for the ancient burial grounds (including planting memorial gardens) has been forthcoming whereas in other locales such as Kalisz Jewish cemeteries have become battlegrounds between advocates and the local governments.

In Kalisz, many of the gravestones from this old cemetery were initially used by the Nazis to reinforce a river embankment. But in 1989, to raise awareness of the desecrated cemetery, the Polish Nissenbaum Foundation, which sponsors several of these restorations, removed a number of gravestones from the river bank to the edge of the sports field. Years later they were moved yet again, this time to a commemorative wall in the city's new Jewish cemetery. And a new law might help honor these Jewish burial grounds. Passed by the Polish Parliament, it grants rights for restitution and supports religious groups' claims to property that remains in government hands.

"It's a classic story," says Chief Rabbi Schudrich. "This older, more historic cemetery was built over by the school, and apartments and a clinic as well." Since the town has moved the students to a new school, he says, this is the logical time to restore and save the cemetery. "But the mayor has stopped the process cold. Instead he wants to put a new school in the old building – and once again over the cemetery. We are not asking them to take down the apartments or the clinic," adds the rabbi. "Just the playground and the now-empty school."

Even with much local support for the excavation and preservation of the cemetery, the mayor still won't consider it, Rabbi Schudrich reports. "In 15 years of working on these issues," he adds, "this is the worst case I have ever seen."

Unfortunately, the rabbi is not surprised. "There's been a lot of heartbreak since the war," he says, listing the pogroms in 1946, official governmental anti-Semitism in 1956 and a prayer found recently in a monastery near Warsaw saying that the Jews should repent to G-d. "And that was post-Vatican II, only a few years ago," he says.

Still, the rabbi says that, like me, he is an optimist about Polish response to Jews and Jewish history. "I believe Jewish life has a chance of flourishing in Poland to a limited extent, especially in larger communities where you have more Jews," he told us. But what about smaller cities like Kalisz? "It's important to strengthen Jewish life where it has a chance, but whether or not any Jews are there now, the city still has a responsibility to preserve the memory of the Jews who once lived there."

———

The Legacy of a Community and a Family

No one knows the exact number but, based on historical evidence, it's likely that no more than 3,000 of the 30,000 Jews who made up a third of Kalisz the summer of 1939 remained alive by the time the Allies liberated Poland six years later. Like my father, each survivor was nothing short of a miracle.

And, like my father, by 1946, just a year after liberation, nearly all of these survivors had gotten as far from Kalisz as they could, to places where they could begin to feel safe and work hard to rebuild their lives.

Where did most of Kalisz's survivors land? Though there were those who chose to stay in Poland, mostly in Warsaw or other big cities, the vast majority ended up in the United States, Canada, Australia, England, France and Israel – and there were those who stayed in the Soviet Union where they had sought sanctuary during the war years (and somehow managed to dodge the anti-Semites there). Wherever they landed, like my parents, they struggled to put the pain of those years behind them and build families and futures for themselves and their children.

But those of us who are their children can tell you it was no simple thing for our parents to put their painful past behind them. Or for us as their children to live with that legacy.

Mindy and I enjoy being with our grandchildren in Jerusalem

As the child of survivors, I grew up mourning them all: My four grandparents, my aunts and uncles and the only first cousin I would ever have. As well as my mother's cousin Jankiel Handelsman who helped plan the Revolt of the Sonderkommandos in October of 1944, to bomb the crematoria in Auschwitz. (This daring plot was immortalized in the film *The Grey Zone*). Along with his other cohorts, Jankiel paid the price for that courage with his life. All of them are almost mythical characters to me, known only by the stories that have come down through my parents, stories I grew up with like other kids grow up with Grimm's fairy tales.

I knew my grandfather Yitzhak Freidenreich in that he refused to surrender his beard and made the sweetest raisin wine for Passover in the ghetto. I knew my grandmother Bayla Kempner in that her chicken soup with flanken was the most delicious my father ever tasted and her skills as a seamstress (like my mother, the daughter-in-law she would never meet) made her an asset to the family embroidery business. And of course I knew my grandfather Mayer Kempner as a passionate Zionist who paid for his dream of a Jewish homeland with the toe the Arabs cut off the night they attacked him standing guard on the kibbutz. The night they warned him to get back to Poland, which he did -- a decision that in a few short years would prove fatal. Hadassah Lesser, my smart-as-a-whip 4-year-old cousin I knew in that a particular Nazi officer had chocolate bars he'd slip to this precocious little daughter of his Jewish dressmaker. Who knows what Hadassah would have done had she not been murdered along with her mom, my clever and courageous Aunt Regina Lesser in the gas chambers of Auschwitz? On her side, only my mom and her sister Frances would live to tell what they'd seen and somehow survived. On my dad's side, besides a few cousins, only he was left to bear witness.

A KEMPNER RETURNS TO KALISZ

My father never had the slightest desire to return to Kalisz. As he used to say, "I have nobody there." Instead, by war's end, he was fully committed to move to Israel (Palestine). But, as soon as he got wind that my mother was alive and living in Kaunitz, Germany, he used every means that a man in love could find – and he was always known for his resourcefulness -- to be reunited with her. Even as an older man, my dad never longed to see his childhood home again. He wasn't sentimental in that way, preferring to treasure that which he had in this happier time of life. In addition, the city of Kalisz where as an only child, he bid farewell to his parents for the last time in the winter of 1940 must have held too many ghosts for him to ever want to see it again. From what I've grown up with, I believe that, for Holocaust survivors, there is no such thing as "closure."

But what my dad didn't need to revisit, I did need to explore for myself.

I'd learned about the significance of Kalisz not only as my father's family home town and one of the oldest cities in Poland, but also the city that first granted civil rights enabling Jews to live in Poland under the protection of the king. Now I wanted to connect with the town and see if they remembered and valued the memory of their lost Jewish community.

So in the spring of 2015, 16 years after my dad's death, I made the trip to Kalisz. It was a strange sensation, walking those streets that a mere 76 years earlier had bustled with Jewish life. With kosher butchers and bakeries selling fresh challah every Friday, with schoolchildren rushing home from *cheder* and peddlers hawking their wares. Only now there is absolutely no sign of any of them, nor is there anyone left to preserve their memory. Except a group of gentile high school kids.

It was these kids, who'd learned about the Jews who once lived here through the Forum for Dialogue who showed me around. On our walking tour of Kalisz's formerly Jewish neighborhoods, the teens pointed out my father's old home (they'd done their homework well before I arrived). They also showed me where the Jewish landmarks had once stood, including the main synagogue where my dad became a bar mitzvah back in 1923, the Torah study halls and mikvehs (ritual baths). These are buildings that exist only in memory today, ghosts of buildings that these kids have learned about from old maps and photos.

As we walked, I was trying to see these streets through the young eyes of my father while at the same time understand how, for these kids, Jewish life here was something they never experienced but could only imagine.

By the end of our day together, they had shared with me what they'd learned and, to my amazement, handed me a copy of my dad's birth certificate and other documents reflecting his early life in Kalisz.

I walked away from my School of Dialogue tour feeling a deep sense of my family's roots and the size and scope of the Kalisz Jewish life that once was. I also came away encouraged that a younger Polish generation was sincerely interested in learning the history of the rise and fall of the Jews of Kalisz.

My Activities and Activism

By then I'd already spent a decade deeply involved in pro-Israel and human rights activism, a passion born after my first visit to Poland in 2005.

After my wife and I had raised our family and I retired from my career as an executive at the Gillette Company, I finally had the time and resources to visit Poland, the land of my parents' birth and formative years. It was in 2005 that I went on my first Adult March of the Living trip. Marking the 60th anniversary of the liberation of Auschwitz, it was an eye-opening, educational and emotional experience to spend the week of Yom Hashoah (Holocaust Memorial Day) in Poland with 25,000 other international visitors and dignitaries. That week I became fascinated with Jewish life in Poland and our family's – and our people's -- history there, a subject that continues to exert a powerful hold on me today.

In the years since my first March of the Living trip, I have been inspired to explore the roots of European antisemitism which ultimately led to the Holocaust and the brutal murders of my grandparents, aunts, uncles and cousins, and to nine out of every 10 Polish Jews.

My mother's hat making skills repeatedly saved her life in the camps. Here my sister Tes models one the thousands of hats our mom has created over the last 75 years

Being in Poland, first in my mother's hometown of Radom and eventually in my dad's native Kalisz, also woke me up to the desperate need for understanding between today's Poles and the Jewish people. For most of the Poles, there was little knowledge (especially among the younger generation) of the

Jews who once lived there as friends and neighbors. But that has begun to change. Wishing to understand their own history since the collapse of the Soviet Union, the Poles have realized that it's impossible to separate the story of the Jews in Poland from Polish history itself.

I believe that, to prevent future Holocausts, we need to build and support bridges of understanding. And I've been increasingly committed to helping strengthen those bridges.

We know from our Torah which teaches us that God let 40 years elapse after the Exodus for the former slave generation to die out before bringing the youngsters who never suffered under Pharaoh's whip into the Promised Land. So we understand why this post-Holocaust bridge of understanding must be built among the young, one heart -- and often one classroom -- at a time.

To raise awareness among our American Jewish youth, for more than a decade each spring I've taken a group of teens on the Road to Remembrance trip to Washington, DC. There we experience the power of the United States Holocaust Memorial Museum and pay our respects at the nearby World War II Memorial. Without the sacrifices of American GIs, our fates may have been very different, I tell them, showing them the 4,000 stars on the "The Price of Freedom Wall" there. Each star represents 100 dead or missing American soldiers. Without them, I tell the kids, my parents and the other remnants of the European Jewry would not have been freed that spring of 1945.

I've also been privileged to help launch and support the Massachusetts chapter of the teen March of the Living (http://motlnewengland.org/), which brings Jewish youth from all over

**Taking teens like these young Americans to the camps
to grasp both the enormity and individual tragedy of the
Holocaust is a great privilege. I believe educating youth
on both sides will help ensure a peaceful future for all**

the world to Poland and Israel to teach them the history of Jews
in Poland and the lessons of the Holocaust.

Our goal: To inspire teens to become community leaders
who will fight hatred and bigotry and promote tolerance and
understanding. I've been privileged to be a docent for both the
teen and adult trips to Poland in recent years and now chair the
March of the Living Massachusetts chapter.

Working with the wonderful people at the Forum for
Dialogue I was also able to sponsor two of their programs, the
first two Schools of Dialogue to take place in 2011 both in my
mom's hometown of Radom and my dad's birthplace of Kalisz

(for more information about the program visit Forum website at www.dialog.org.pl). My hope and prayer is that by increasing understanding between us and raising awareness among the upcoming generation about the Jews who once lived there we will prevent the kind of prejudice and distrust that led to the Holocaust in the first place.

To help ensure that the understanding is flowing freely in both directions, I have accompanied groups of American Jewish kids on the March of the Living trips and Polish gentile teenagers and educators through the Forum's School of Dialogue programs.

With School of Dialogue participants, saying goodbye in front of their high school

Thanks in great part to the vision and commitment of those associated with the Forum for Dialogue, there are now many in the modern Polish city of Kalisz who are working hard at making peace with its past. I deeply believe that my father would be pleased and proud to know that he and his family and friends have not been forgotten. I believe he would be as hopeful as I am that these kids from Kalisz want to learn about their city's Jewish past and that their community is supporting the School of Dialogue program. This attitude, I firmly believe, is the only way we can hope to build a future of tolerance and true respect.

It has been my distinct honor through my activism and now through this book to bear witness to the life of my father David Kempner, to his family and friends and the entire Jewish community of Kalisz. To the beautiful world they created, one that not only strengthened and inspired them for generations but also that enhanced the lives of their Polish neighbors during their 800 years there. And to their courage and strength under the most horrible of circumstances. May their memory be for a blessing.

---- **Irv Kempner,** January 8, 2018

<u>"Yizkor"</u>

May God remember the souls of our brethren of Israel who

Resided in the City of Kalisz and became martyrs and heroes

During the Holocaust: thirty thousand Jews who were slain, murdered,

Strangled and buried alive, the entire holy congregation of Kalisz

Who were destroyed and hallowed the Name.

May God remember how they were offered up with the other martyrs and heroes of Israel since time untold

And may their souls be bound up in the bonds of life.

They were lovely and pleasant in their lives,

And in their death they were not divided.

May they rest in peace where they lie.

And let us say....Amen.

-- ***Kalisz Memorial Book***